What Marie Did Next.....

Tina M Piper

This book is a work of fiction. Even though the book is based on true events in the authors life, all names, characters, places and incidents are used fictitiously and any resemblance to any actual persons, living or dead, events or places are entirely coincidental.

INTRODUCTION

Although I am, at the time of publication of this book, only 51 years old, my life so far has been full to say the least. I consider myself one of those people who stuff just happens to......... that, events in another woman's life might be catastrophic but somehow I deal with them.................... I would say I am definitely someone who takes each and every opportunity given and runs with it good or bad.

Maybe that's my military upbringing? As a Pad Brat and subsequent army wife I can hear the voice in my head saying "You'll just have to get on with it!" and I certainly had to!

I consider myself to be very fortunate in the life I have led. Sure, it's had its very dark times, very very dark times which you will read about but also I have had really great, hilariously funny, uplifting and special times.

This book has been a labour of love. Some of the dark events were so hard to revisit as I had buried them, especially with reference to my first husband, my children's father, who, whilst I have been writing this book has died. A little nod to you J. I hope you are no longer the troubled soul we knew.

So, as I sit here embarking on a new adventure (which will be in the sequel................) I feel lucky, fortunate and blessed. They say everyone has a book in them. Once I started writing mine, I certainly did!

I hope you, the reader can see why I wrote this.

Enjoy the ride...........................

ACKNOWLEDGMENTS

I would like to thank my wonderful husband who copes with the events that seem to surround my existence with patience and a resigned "Yes Dear........" Without you D, none of this would be possible or achievable. You saved me at perhaps the lowest point in my life. You are my life. A large part of this book is about my children and my grandson, without you guys this book would have a gaping hole in it so thanks for being here lol xxx

Thanks go to all of my Pad Brat friends who I grew up with in 3rd Battalion, Royal Regt. of Fusiliers and in my joint unit schools in West Germany, especially you my oldest friend D. You all remain my anchors! We all have a special connection us military kids and I, for one am so happy my dad joined the Army just because of that! Thanks to social media we can all find each other and continue to connect and grow. Also to my fellow 1st Battalion Kings Own Scottish Borderers wives W and L. You know who you are and you probably don't realise what a support you were to me in Berlin and Edinburgh!

G in Bali, thank you so much.

Thanks to you the reader! I hope you enjoy this book. This project was intended for you to be able to read it and enjoy it, so please do!

Writer Unknown

So So True........................

This is……………………

What Marie Did Next….

CHAPTERS

CHANCE MEETING 1
GETTING STARTED 12
DISCOVERING ROOTS 22
CHILDHOOD 32
GROWING UP 51
FIRST LOVE 67
MEETING JACK 79
MARRIED LIFE 96
FIRST BORN 104
BERLIN 'FAMILY' LIFE 113
A SCOTTISH NIGHTMARE 124
BABIES, AFFAIRS AND A PRINCESS 134
THE FINAL STRAW... OR NOT 150
CIVVY STREET 160
UNREASONABLE BEHAVIOUR 171
OFF THE RAILS 182
THE MAN OF MY DREAMS 193
MORE UPS AND DOWNS 211
DUNGEON MASTER AND MISTRESS 221
TRIALS AND TRIBULATIONS 237
EMAILS 257
NEW BEGINNINGS 266
EPILOGUE: FIVE YEARS LATER 273

CHANCE MEETING

The night I met Marie I got exceptionally drunk for the first time in about ten years; but that was my fault not hers. The reason I subjected myself to a terrible hangover the next day was because, for the first time in that same period, I truly let my hair down and totally and utterly enjoyed 'life'.

That was the affect she had on me and that's why she's still such a good friend now; she just brings out the real me when I have trouble letting go on my own. I'm not going to talk about myself too much, but I will go so far as to say I went a bit quiet socially after a very stressful divorce. The thing is, this book is not about me; this is Marie's story and I can honestly say her life is *much* more interesting than mine.

It's a much abused phrase, but Marie really is one of those people who lights up a room when she walks into it. Some people are so miserable they can suck out all the good vibes from others instantly, absolute fun sponges; Marie is a mood-hoover too, but in the best possible sense. She takes away your doubts and depressions and fills the space with laughter and the simple joy of life.

But the thing that makes Marie's story so interesting is that her life has not always been like that; far, far from it; it's a life of real extremes. That's why I felt compelled to write it down; all that I'm going to tell you about her really happened. There will be laughter and there will be tears but then, without all that, there wouldn't be Marie.

Let me get myself out of the way first and then we can get on with Marie's story. My name is Tina Piper and I'm an author; but hopefully you've worked that out already. I'll admit to being 40 years old and well, you already know I'm divorced. In fact I've been man-free since I got rid of my leech of a husband and my life has been wonderfully quiet. I started writing properly when I was in my late twenties when an unexpected inheritance from my Grandmother allowed me to stop having to work in a paid position for my money and pursue my dream of writing.

The first book I wrote was an awful romance, but I managed to get the second in front of literary agent; she told me the truth; it was, to use her phrase, a load of crap! But the way she told me never hurt me for a second because what she did do was point out the good bits, there weren't many but they were something to build on; she sent me away to try again. I did and the next book sold 100,000 copies.

Well that was four books ago and now I was taking a well-earned break after nine months on the latest one. I had taken myself off to Bali for an extended holiday and after I stayed in the south in Seminyak for a few days I moved north. I ended up in an area called The Lovina and checked in at a brand new resort.

That night I went to get a drink before dinner. Situated between the pool and the beach was a square-shaped bar, with seating via high stools on three sides. Only one person was there, a dark looking woman who I decided looked distinctly Italian. I thought I'd go take a look at the beach before sitting down and was making my way past the woman when a barman started walking back towards the hotel. He stopped to wait for me to get past but I still managed to walk too close to the woman and tripped over the hand bag she'd left on the floor.

"Oh mi scusi mi dispiace" I said, apologising in the few bits of Italian I remembered from school as I quickly grabbed at the bar to stop myself falling flat on my face. The woman jumped at first in surprise and then reached out a hand to steady me.

"Non è un problema" she replied as she laughed and slipped off her stool to help me restore the contents of her bag; the barman was picking up bits that had scattered under a nearby table. We got her purse and phone and bits of make-up put away and then I must have raised an eyebrow as I handed her a small packet of latex-free condoms. She grinned.

"Oh, mi dispiace. Una ragazza deve stare attento!" I manage to translate that as 'I'm sorry' and 'a girl's got to be careful'.

I just smiled with her and wished I could be as confident in myself as she was, my Italian certainly didn't stretch to a conversation about her sex life. We thought we'd got everything when we realised that the barman was standing there with what I thought at first was a gold lipstick.

"You have this madam," he said in his limited English, holding it out to the woman and she said thank you and quickly took it off him.

"Oh bugger!" she whispered as she pushed it into her bag; her accent as Northern English as you could get.

"You're English?" I said with a laugh.

"Yes love I am and your Italian accent is crap!"

I couldn't have taken offence at this, the way she said it was just so funny. The fact that we'd had a such a stupid mix up after my clumsiness and her being able to just speak like that to someone she'd only just met broke the ice completely. Then she added:

"Trust it to be him that has to pick up my bloody finger vibrator!"

We both cracked up laughing.

"I can't believe he did that!" she said with a sheepish grin.

"Well I don't think he knew what it was" I replied.

"Don't you be so sure after last night" she whispered, looking at my face for a response.

She must have achieved exactly the reaction she was looking for since I'm sure my eyebrows were in danger of disappearing into my hairline. She burst out laughing:

"Don't worry love, I'm not that bad!" she said as she restored the offending item to the safety of her bag and bent her head to straighten everything up inside it.

I gave up the idea of looking at the beach, choosing instead to take a seat at the bar. I ordered a glass of Sauvignon-Blanc and when it came I toasted the woman who raised her own glass, an exotic looking cocktail. I guessed her to be about the same age as me and she had thick, long brown hair, pushed back from a wrinkle-free forehead and bright hazel eyes beneath perfectly arched eyebrows; I can never get mine to look that good. Her lovely Cupid's bow mouth was delicately coloured and looked like a one of those perfectly shaped, small mouths of the cartoon heroine. She was wearing a black chiffon vest top and matching trousers and her figure? Before I wrote this I looked up the definition in the dictionary: 'very attractive with strong sex appeal, large breasts and appealing curves'. She was the walking definition of voluptuous.

With my short, blonde bob and 34A chest I felt decidedly inferior, but had immediately decided I liked this woman. She had an alluring look that would certainly attract any man but perhaps she could be seen as a threat for a jealous type woman. To me her smile was pure warmth; with a definite hint of mischief. After a few moments she looked up again and took a drink as she seemed to realise I was still alone.

"Your husband not 'ere yet?" she said in that accent. I learnt later that Marie had moved from Scotland and now lived in London. So I was intrigued as to where that accent was actually from.

I shook my head:

"No, I'm on my own" I replied before taking another sip of wine.

"Oh me too," she said and then laughed gently as she caught the eye of the young Balinese barman now back at his post; he smiled before looking away, clearly embarrassedly. She then added:

"That's why I need my little gold friend!" she said before laughing again. Then she added:

"Mind you it's a bit quiet here and not quite like Malaga where you get trampled to death by Spanish waiters wanting to get your knickers off!"

Just the way she came out with it made me laugh. There was nothing lewd about the comment, just a simple statement of the facts delivered with a mischievous grin.

"Not that I'm looking for a bloke that is" she continued with a slight shake of her head. There was something in that small gesture that told of troubles in the past, but I was not going to pry. That came later but only when she wanted to talk to me; there really was a lot to pry into!

"Me neither," I replied with a smile, "I've lasted ten years without so I'll carry on as I am thank you!"

She laughed.

"Good for you girl! I've got a man but I left him at home to do the washing and ironing!"

If I'd been taking a drink at the time I think I would have snorted it back down my nose; she just had a great way with words and I later realised that I had already started to subconsciously store them away to be written down later. I guess I was thinking about making her a character in a book; she became much more than that.

"The condoms are for him in case he gets caught short and wants to do it in the car!"

I must have looked shocked and she burst out laughing.

"Sorry love, I'm only joking, we'd had a night away together before I came out here" she explained and then reached out a hand.

"My name's Marie" she said and I reached over and shook it. Not a bone-crunching macho grip like a bloke, but a good, solid and meaningful handshake which I returned; I really was pleased to meet her.

"I'm Tina, Tina Piper." I said.

She looked at me for a moment and then lifted a beautifully manicured and polished nail to her lips.

"Not the author? New Brooms and After Tinker?"

I nodded and smiled, embarrassed as always when I create a sense of 'being famous'. She had named the first book and the one before last,

"That's me, but I'm here incognito" I whispered.

She laughed out loud.

"Oh your secret's safe with me!" she said with a wink, "I'll just say I love your books and then we'll move on to talk about the best way to murder a man once you've maxed his credit card!"

She was so on my wavelength and with only half a glass of wine I was in danger of getting the giggles.

"Thank you for that and I'd say that's a much better conversation. I'd just like to know how to get the credit card without having to put up with the snoring and the toilet seat being left up!"

"Oh too right" she said after she'd finished her cocktail and signalled for another.

"One guy once said to me he was going to make me the happiest woman in the world. So you know what I replied?"

I shook my head.

"I'll miss you for a while!" she replied and before I could stop laughing she leaned forward and said in a quieter voice.

"Did you know that it was supposed to be Cleopatra that invented the vibrator?"

I shook my head, actually intrigued.

"Yeah apparently she had a solid gold metal tube that was filled with angry bees!"

"She did what?" I laughed incredulous.

"Well yeah, so the story goes. Can you just imagine it? Mark Anthony walks in with a big 'I'm really pleased to see you' lump under his toga and she says buzz off I'm busy!"

And so it went on as I had another glass of wine and we talked about my thinking she was Italian and she laughed gently and said it happened quite often and she told me it was a long story. Then we thought we'd better eat something and went and sat at a table on the beach and cemented our friendship over bowls of pasta and bottle of Cabernet-Merlot. She told me that my assumption had been correct in that some women found her threatening; she had few female friends; I was glad that I might become one of them. I was already more mellow than I'd been in a long while and it was still only 9:00pm. She had that effect.

Over dinner I learnt that she was in fact 51, she certainly didn't look it, and then the conversation did get a little more serious for a while as we turned to the subject of husbands; she was on number two and she gave me hints of the first that made me shudder inside. She wanted to know all about mine so I told her a few bits about how I named him the leech because he just clung to me until I felt smothered; I told her I knew he'd hate the idea of me writing and so that was part of my decision to pursue it. She laughed out loud at the description of him as a blood-sucker in M&S y-fronts.

"Oh I know just the type" she said as put her fork down for a moment and pointed her index finger in the air as if she were about to explain some scientific theory, "I bet he used to take his trousers off before his shoes and socks and still think he used to look sexy?"

"Oh worse!" I said with a grin, "he'd take the baggy y-fronts off as well before the shoes and socks!"

"Oh gross!" she replied and laughed so loud she caused the few other diners that were now near us to look around.

But later on she told me a few much, much worse stories than that; some which caused hilarity and some which brought tears to my eyes. After dinner we had gone for brief walk along the beach and this did clear my head a little before we went back to the bar and she got me started on the cocktails! It was after about the third of these that I knew I had to soon stop but they had given me courage to speak to her about some of the ideas already forming in my head. She had such a strong personality it was an author's dream, the kind that would only normally be made up. But here she was, as real as can be and as totally full of life as someone 25 years younger.

"This stuff you've told me, I'd imagine there's even more of your, what shall I say, major life experiences?"

She laughed once more and shook her head briefly.

"Oh tons more and a lot worse! In fact, you could write a bloody book about it all!"

It was clear she'd been joking and playing on the fact of my being a writer. I swallowed, took a deep breath and plunged in.

"Well actually... that's what I was thinking..." I said, more quietly than we'd been talking up to this point.

She was just about to take a drink of her cocktail and she stopped her arm dead with the glass only half way to her mouth. She looked at me for a moment and her eyes met mine and then she put the glass back down, the drink untouched.

"Oh bloody hell! You're serious aren't you?" she asked; her voice almost a whisper.

I simply nodded and waited whilst she considered what I'd said.

"You mean you want the whole warts n'all, no holds barred, kick in the balls story?"

"Yes I do" I said, hoping this was actually going the way I thought it was,

"There's some real... err... controversial stuff in there that most people would run a mile from..."

She left the point open as a form of question and I leaned forward, signalling my clear and serious interest.

"I guessed as much and you've already certainly opened my eyes, but what I'd be looking for is how it impacted you; not so much about what happened in detail, but why and how. I'd want to write about the relationships and the characters around you that caused your life to move in certain directions."

She now took a sip of her drink as she mulled over what I had said, clearly scrolling through some of the stories in her mind like flicking through pages in a book as she captured an image here and there. Then she nodded gently.

"There's some very dark stuff but..." she said and then her face lit up again as she paused briefly before grinning again with a real wicked look in her eyes, "there's some bloody hilarious things as well!"

I smiled and stayed silent; I wanted her to carry on thinking it through. She suddenly looked more serious again.

"But who would be interested in my story?"

"I've been speaking to you for a couple of hours and I want to know all of it already!", I replied.

I paused before saying anything else and held my breath and then she nodded.

"Well I think I'll agree to it, but I need to sleep on it as well and ask you some more tomorrow when I'm not pissed! But for now, yeah I think it might just go along with it. A book about my life eh? Well who would have thought it?"

Inside I actually wanted to dance and jump around, but I smiled and picked up my glass and held it out to hers.

"You can't say fairer than that; but I won't let you down." I said with a somewhat drunken grin.

"Oh I'm sure you won't" she replied and then downed the remainder of her cocktail as if it were juice. "So let's have another drink to celebrate and fairs fair, I now want to know lots more about *your* dark and sordid past Tina Piper!"

GETTING STARTED

We finally went to be bed around midnight and I had a quick shower to get rid of the sand from my feet and other places — I mean how does it get in there? I was full of good, OK drunken, intentions and planned on setting my alarm for eight the next day; I have no idea if I forgot to turn it on or whether I slept through it but I eventually surfaced around 9:30am. At the time I was only just feeling capable of leaving my room and I was surprised to find Marie already by the pool; a few drops of water on her skin told of a recent swim. Then I remembered through the haze in my befuddled brain that this was her last day and that she has said she wanted to make the most of it; she was obviously more organised than I was after a long night. But she was lying on sun-lounger under an umbrella whilst wearing dark glasses, even though the day was a little cloudy; perhaps she did feel as bad as me but I had sunglasses on too. There was pot of coffee, an empty cup and an empty juice glass on the table beside her.

"Well well! Younger than me and the last to get up!" she said with a grin as she noticed me walking over.

"Oh don't" I said as I sat on the edge of the bed next to hers, "I may be younger but I've been out of drinking practice for a long time! My mouth feels like it's full of dead fish!"

She laughed as she sat up and poured me a coffee into the spare cup she'd organised.

"There's never any sympathy for self-inflicted injuries" she said passing me the life-line I so very much needed. I took the cup from her gratefully.

"I do feel there's an element of blame on your part because wasn't it your idea that I switch to those lethal cocktails?" I said in between sips of coffee.

She laughed again and pushed her glasses up onto her head; her eyes didn't look half as bad as mine.

"Well perhaps I did make the suggestion but you didn't need too much encouragement!" she teased.

I sipped some more coffee, it was only luke warm but it did make things better; slightly. I dared to lift up my own glasses; it was darker under the umbrella.

"Actually, I haven't enjoyed myself like that in a long, long time and so maybe I should even thank you for this wonderful pain I am suffering and for my stomach feeling like it's been mangled by some demented alien that's taken over my body!"

She laughed out loud again and actually slapped me on the thigh.

"Oh you crack me up, you really do! There you are with your school teacher hair do and your prim and proper ways and beneath all that there's this St.Trinians' girl desperate to escape!"

Coming from anyone else it could have been mildly hurtful, but not from Marie. I just had to grin and realised she'd made me feel better already. Eventually we ordered some toast for breakfast and then mostly lost ourselves in the books we were reading and I dozed for a while. There was no mention of my biography ideas until we began to walk along the beach later to go into the nearby village to get some lunch.

"I've been thinking about the book," she said, as we splashed our feet gently in the shallow, crystal clear water, "and I'm still up for the idea, but I need to talk to my husband first. He knows all about my life before I met him of course but, as much as we might disguise things, there are going to be people who might read it and know it's me and I don't want it to cause any problems. Is that OK?"

"Of course it is" I replied, "I know he was great about you taking this break by yourself and so you don't want to go back and say: 'Hiya luv', I met an author on 'oliday and I'm goin' to do a kiss n'tell book about me life; OK?'"

She laughed out loud and hit me on the arm.

"You might be great with words Tina bloody Piper but that's the worst fake Northern accent I've ever heard! Worse than the Italian!"

"Ouch!" I said rubbing my arm, "and it wasn't *that* bad!" Actually I knew it was terrible and also I will say that most of the time there's only a trace of Marie's roots in the way she speaks; it just came out more when she was drunk. My badly delivered impression was not just a sign of my now feeling more alive than I'd done a couple of hours previously, but it also told how much I could relax and really be myself in her company.

"Seriously, of course I understand that and there's also the fact that I've got to speak to Liz my agent to see what she thinks of the ideas as well; she's the one that will have to sell it to my publisher. But I'm sure she'll trust my judgment."

"Well that's alright then" she said as we came off the beach when we saw the first signs of the bars and restaurants. Marie led to me a small warung, an Indonesian cafe that she'd been to before. Run by a lovely woman called Ayu and her daughter, Marie said the food was cheap and simple but everything was freshly cooked. We both ordered some mango juice and Nasi Goreng, the traditional Indonesia fried rice and settled back in our chairs to relax and watch the world go by. As well as other tourists going past, there were lots of locals as well, like the woman who came to the warung with a big metal bowl balanced on her head. She took it down and her and Ayu bartered loudly over the price of some fish; this was the Bali I had been looking for. Marie had come here to Lovina as a first choice and had wondered, after the long journey from the airport in the South, if she had made the wrong decision. I told her she hadn't at all.

"So before you speak to your agent is there anything else you need to know?" she asked as we began to eat our food, it was really delicious and the whole meal for both of was going to cost less than a fiver. This was about half the price of the food in Seminyak or Ubud, as cooked by the locals that is; in restaurants and hotels the price was not far off those back in the UK.

"No I don't think so" I said, after another drink of the delicious, freshly prepared juice.

"I'm sure that I have more than enough to convince myself that it's very much worth doing and

I'm sure that will be enough for Liz to think so too. But what about your husband? How is he going to feel?"

"Oh I reckon he'll be fine, I just don't want to present it to him as a done deal. I will tell him that I'm thinking about it and ask his opinion. Whatever I want to do he's very supportive... I'm very lucky."

Those last few words, spoken a little more quietly and with deep affection, almost seemed to show a different side to Marie that spoke of her not always having the brash confidence she seemed to portray most of the time now; I was to learn later she'd been painfully shy as a teenager. But the words clearly showed that she was happy and contented now and I was pleased for her; especially after some of the things she had mentioned last night. But as she had said a number of times, we'd only scratched the surface for now and I was itching to get started.

***

And so we did. Whilst Marie was back in the UK talking to her husband, I had a couple of Skype calls on my iPad with Liz and after I told her the essentials of the story and my ideas for writing it she was immediately as keen as I was. The next day, about two hours after she had sent me an email telling me the publishers said go ahead (and would give me an even bigger advance than usual!) it all came together when I got an email from Marie; she said her husband John was very supportive. So I emailed her back straight away and said how pleased and excited I was and we agreed to meet first at for our first session a few days later; it was fortunate we both lived in London.

By now my time in the north of this beautiful place called Bali could feasibly come to an end. I had seen endless rice fields when I had gone to visit the wonderful waterfalls in the mountains in the village of Gitgit and I had been diving on the coral off Menjangan Island and so I was happy to cut my holiday short by a few days. I changed my flight and the next day I flew back to the UK via Kuala Lumpur. One week after that the doorbell sounded on my flat in Fulham and I buzzed Marie in. I was only dressed in clothes for being lazy at home, but Marie came in looking fabulous in some designer jeans tucked into black boots and a soft tan coloured leather jacket over a dark navy polo neck. Her hair shone beautifully and put my dull locks totally to shame; I made a mental note to book in with my hairdresser. We made some coffee and then, with a tape machine set up on the coffee table, our work together began.

"So let's start with the basic facts then" I said, new notebook on my knee.

Whilst I had the tape going I would also want to jot down points I needed to come back to without interrupting her all the time. I also wanted to make a note of things that struck me as most important or things that could impact her in later life. As she crossed and uncrossed her legs a couple of times, Marie actually looked nervous at first, but we soon settled into a rhythm.

She was born Marie Louise Turner on 19th April 1960 in Bolton Royal Infirmary, Greater Manchester to parents Michael and Patricia Turner....

"Fifteen months after I was born my brother Andrew came along then nearly two years after him my sister Helen. My parents were dead young when they had me; Mum was twenty two and Dad was only just turned twenty."

She paused to get a drink of coffee and I went to get her a glass of water; my mouth would have been dry too in her situation. Then she laughed briefly.

"It was when I was 15 and we were discussing their wedding anniversary being on mum's birthday that I realised my Mum was pregnant with me when she walked down the aisle with Dad! They were married the previous year, a bit before Christmas. Most people in Bolton in those days still worked in one of the cotton mills but Dad worked on the railway, fixing the track and stuff like that. Mum used to work in a Clark's shoe shop and they met when Dad went in for some new winkle-pickers, he was a bit of a Mod in those days!"

She paused then and looked like she needed a bit of a prompt:

"What about your parents' families and your grandparents?" I asked.

"Oh right, yeah. Well Mum is the youngest of five sisters, but Dad is an only child. I don't have much to do with my Aunties. I never knew my maternal Granddad as he died when I was a baby and, well... I guess likewise for my paternal one also. Well at least who I thought was Dad's Dad!"

"What do you mean?" I asked, making the first note in my book. She laughed.

"Oh I'll tell you that one later!" she said with grin before carrying on. She seemed much more relaxed now.

"So where was I? Oh yeah. Both my Grandmas were wonderful. Both are gone to a better place now, but they were both just adorable, just like every child's vision of the perfect Grandma. My

Mum's Mum used to be always singing and I still can hear her voice in my head, singing away to herself in that trilling tone as she did her ironing! She died when she was quite old and I would be about 27; I know my Mum has never really got over losing her. She had snow white hair and smelled of talcum powder and made me feel loved and safe. I loved her very much. My dad never called her anything but Mrs Rudd out of total respect for her. She was so kind and loving."

Apart from her comments about her husband, this was my first real hint of emotion in Marie and I waited whilst she dabbed at her eyes with a tissue she pulled from her bag. I wrote down 'talcum powder' in my book; it was such a meaningful description. She smiled but said nothing about the interruption.

"But my Dad's Mum, Grandma Alice, she was actually my beloved grandma and I loved her so much it hurt. She loved me too and I know I was her favourite... the reasons for that will come clear later when I talk about Dad's Dad. Grandma Alice had a brother, Joe and a sister, Florence, who she was always with when she went shopping or went to bingo. Grandma Alice featured a lot in our lives when she was married to her second hubby Stan. That's part of the same story about Dad's Dad.

"I can't remember much up until when I must have been getting on for five years old, and my sister must have been quite small still, but I remember at the back of our house in Bolton on Broad Street there was a bit of waste land which seemed huge to us kids back then and we used to play all sorts of games there. I've since been back there and actually it's very small! Across the other side of the waste land was a church with a big steeple and

I remember the stained glass windows; they were just beautiful when the sun was shining on them and I just used to sit cross-legged on old grave-stone and just stare at them ..."

Already I was sitting enthralled just hearing her talk like that and I longed to tell her she should write herself, she had such a lovely way with words that seemed to flow naturally; this book was going to be great. She finished her coffee and then laughed at a memory.

"I never really knew why, but there were always empty car transporters parked nearby, loads of them really and to us kids, as young as we were, they were just a magnet! One perfect summer's day, my brother climbed on one right to the top and I told him to be careful, but of course he went and fell off! He was a bit battered and bruised and the worst was where his split his ear open and there was blood everywhere; I remember this older girl fainted! I know I was convinced that Mum would blame me for not looking after him but she didn't go off on one or panic at all; she just dealt with it and patched him up.

"Another memory from this time was an old lady called Betty who didn't live far from us and Mum used to take us to visit. I've no idea if she was related somehow or just an older lady Mum liked, but she was really lovely. She adored my long dark hair and wanted to brush it all the time and basically, she just spoiled me rotten with sweets and her old jewellery. I know she was older but she had peroxide blonde hair in an enormous beehive and bright blue eyes. She wore twin sets and kitten heels."

She paused then and looked at the clock on her iPhone.

"Right, I'm starving after all that talking and I need a drink. Go and get changed and you can buy me lunch and I'll tell you all about Stan."

I was to learn that this was Marie.................. spontaneous and always thinking ahead!

DISCOVERING ROOTS

It was mid-week and quiet anyway, but we walked round the corner from my flat to wine bar I knew wouldn't be really that busy so there wouldn't be lots of noise to cause problems on the tape later. If any extraneous words were picked up they would be edited out when the tapes were transcribed; these files would then become the basis for the book. I knew Marie and her husband ran a restaurant in Islington and I saw her giving the place a good look over. It had recently had an expensive refurbishment.

"This place doesn't look too bad" said Marie as she sipped her white wine. "What's the food like?"

"Bistro-ish" I replied and she nodded before I added:

"So what kind of food do you like?"

"Well our restaurant's, to use your words, bistro-ish I guess. I don't like what I call 'posh' food where you get some tiny morsel in the middle of the plate with a few drops of something fancy strategically drizzled on the side with an edible flower and what the bloody hell is that foam stuff all about?"

"You mean like you get in McDonalds?" I asked and she laughed.

"Yeah right! Gary Rhodes designer ketchup! I like what I'd call decent-posh that has some imagination and some good flavours but doesn't leaving you starving for a Big Mac when you've finished it and it hasn't cost you a bloody fortune."

At that point, we turned to the menus and both settled for fish, sea bream for me and mussels for Marie. We talked a bit more about favourite foods and the menu in her restaurant then she brought us back to her story. As we walked from the flat I'd asked her how she felt about the first session; strange but exciting was how she described it.

"So where did we get to?" she asked.

"You were going to satisfy my curiosity about Stan" I reminded her.

"Oh yeah... Stan..."

She took a sip of wine and I let her gather her thoughts. For a moment she looked like a school girl stuck on her homework. Then she gave me one of those grins.

"Right here we go... Before I was born and even before Mum and Dad started 'courting' as Dad used to call it, he thought his Dad's name was Jim Turner..."

She put her glass down and leaned forward, putting her elbows on the table and steepling her fingers; to me a clear sign of her serious mood. I added the name of Jim Turner next to the Stan I had written earlier; I sensed a connection coming and I wasn't wrong. Her use of the word 'thought' was intriguing.

"Now, none of us in our generation ever met Jim because when my Dad was in the merchant navy when he was 16, Jim died. Dad was away in the South China Seas and so never got back for the funeral. You know, it was funny because Dad never spoke about this, ever. As we grew up we were just told that Granddad Turner had died. We never learnt anything about him and Grandma never spoke of him either; no pictures, nothing. We three kids accepted that Stan was married to Grandma and thought of him as our Granddad although we never called him that, he was just lovable Stan to us."

She paused again, clearly at a point where the story moved on; it was then that the waitress brought our food. We started on our meals and had the usual "mine's nice—yours nice?" conversation and both agreed we were quite happy. After Marie had carefully arranged some mussel shells like a display around her bowl she continued.

"One day when I was fifteen there was just me and Mum in the house; I'd been ill and was still off school. Andrew and Helen had left for school as usual and Dad was at work. After we'd had some lunch, beans on toast it was and I always remember that because I'd not really eaten for a few days and it was one of my favourites then, she sat me down and told me something that had been a major cause of upset in the family, especially for my Grandma Alice. I found out later that Grandma was really upset that Mum had told me and subsequently Andy and Helen."

She paused for a few moments for a drink and more food and then continued:

"Well now, it turned out that Stan had met Grandma Alice when my Mum was pregnant with me. Now here's where it gets strange. For some reason that I guess I will never know because Grandma is dead now, Stan hired a private detective to look into Grandma's life."

"Why on earth would he do that?" I interrupted.

"Apparently he'd heard a rumour that, going back to just after the war had finished, she'd had a one night stand with an Italian prisoner of war who had been housed in a camp on Saddleworth Moor; he was on a night out in Bolton..."

She paused but I didn't interrupt. I now knew why she looked like she did. Dark. European almost.

"So there you have it. My Dad was half Italian and Jim Turner was not his real father."

"So when did Jim come into the picture? Was that after your Dad was born or what?" I asked

"Apparently Jim had loved my Grandma from afar in the cotton mill they both worked in when they were young, but he was a shy kind of character apparently and had never spoken to her about his feelings, even though they lived near each other as well and used to speak a little bit in the street. Anyway, somehow he found out she was pregnant with my Dad and bless him he whisked her off to Yorkshire and married her. He got some work locally there for a while and after my Dad was born they came back to Bolton as a family unit with supposedly no one any the wiser that Jim wasn't the baby's real father."

"He must have loved her very much I guess, but did your Grandmother love him?" I asked.

"Oh for sure he did but as for her, I don't know really if she did or not, but I know she was very grateful to him. It's maybe more acceptable, in fact bloody normal to have a kid on your own now, but back in 1945, even amongst working class people, it was still a big no-no."

"I'm sure" I answered as we both finished our meal. Then I asked:

"But what about Stan when he found all this out?"

"Well apparently he'd said nothing at first but then he asked my Dad to go for a pint with him. They settled down with their drinks and Stan presented Dad with this a brown envelope; in it was the Private Detective's report. Of course my Dad had absolutely no idea about any of this, Grandma and Grandad Jim had decided he wasn't to know and as far as he was concerned Jim was his Dad."

"Oh my God Marie! That must have been awful for your Dad." I said when she'd stopped. She nodded in agreement as she sipped the last of her wine and then continued the story as she put her glass back on the table.

"Well yeah. As you can imagine, here we have a man just turned twenty with a new wife who's already pregnant with their first child. He was devastated by the whole thing because not only did Stan give him this report from the private dick, he went on to say that he *and* Grandma never wanted to see him, his wife or the Italian bastard child—meaning me—she was carrying ever again!"

"I mean..........can you imagine?" she said, her eyes wide and her hands upturned, so very Italian.

Before I spoke I just drew a series of exclamation marks after the word Stan in my notebook. This was already like something from a made up drama on TV but instinctively I knew this was a true reflection of that period in time. I was absolutely transfixed by her story.

"But what did your Grandma say about all this? She can't have agreed with what Stan said to your Dad, her only son... surely?"

"Apparently Mum and Dad didn't see her up until I was about 9 weeks old. They had tried to see Grandma, but Stan was very strong character and he more or less kept her prisoner. Mum thought that he'd harboured a real grudge or even been jealous about Grandma Alice and this Italian and once he let it out by telling my Dad he kind of flipped. Even her brother and sister were not allowed to see her."

The waitress came over and we both ordered coffee and Marie asked for a glass of water and then she carried on.

"Anyway, Mum and Grandma had always got on and Mum was convinced it was all Stan's doing so one day she decided she'd had enough and she went round to their house. From the photographs I have of when I was a baby I looked very much like my Dad, quite dark skinned with head full of very dark hair and Mum knew my Grandma would love me so much. She told me that when my other lovely Grandma, her mum came to see me for the first time in hospital she declared "Well I never! There is no denying whos daughter she is.........you couldn't deny that!" looking straight at my dad.

Mum put me in my Silver Cross pram with my best dress on and when Stan answered the door she just shoved him out of the way and went in; Mum's only quite small and Stan was about 6′ 2″! She'd done all this off her own bat by the way; my Dad was at work and had no idea what she was up to."

"I can see where you get your strength of character from" I said with a grin and she laughed.

"Oh bloody hell yes, Mum's a fighter alright!" she agreed but then got more serious again.

"Anyway, she told me that what she saw in that house could only be described as horrific. She said my Grandma, who was tiny anyway, was sat in a chair, she was very thin and gaunt looking. Of course Stan kicked off shouting at Mum to get that Italian bastard, me of course, out of his house and never to come back, but Mum just ignored him. She gently placed me in Grandma's arms proudly saying 'This is your new granddaughter Marie Louise'..."

She paused for a moment to drink some water as the coffee was served; I detected a glisten of tears in her eyes, but she didn't reach for a tissue from her bag. Then she smiled:

"I suppose you can now see why I was her favourite out of all three of her grandkids."

"I'll bet you were. So what happened next?" I asked.

"Oh well of course there were tears and hugs but Stan was having none of it and with my Grandma sobbing her heart out he threw Mum and me out of the house. Now I'm not quite sure what happened then, but Grandma started coming to see Mum and Dad and me in our little house on her own and in secret. My Mum said how hard up her and Dad were and described Grandma bringing them bits of money stuffed inside old envelopes and pushing these into my Mum's hand. This must have gone on for some time as my brother had come along and Mum was bedridden and ill with her pregnancy with Helen. There were stories of my Grandma coming to help out every day while Dad was working.

"Later on Stan became part of our lives and I think the start of it began with a tale of Grandma and Stan visiting us all and Grandma saying: 'I'll just nip to the loo before we set off home' and went out of the room. Apparently when she and Stan got home he said that he knew she had been going to our house in secret because she knew exactly where the loo was!"

"So did things get better after that?" I asked.

"Well yeah because I was still too young to remember any of the problems and us kids always thought Stan was great. He treated us lovely and was never different to me despite what he'd thought when I was born."

"But what happened to sort it all out?"

"Well, from what I understand, what happened was that Dad eventually had a real go at Stan and this was around the time he decided to join the Army, which was when I was five or a bit after. Apparently Frank apologised to Dad and after that he let Auntie Flo and Uncle Joe back into Grandma's life again. Something must have happened to make him a better person because us kids really loved him, especially my brother and we were of course oblivious to what had gone on when I was born. When Mum told me all about it she said that underneath it all she hated Stan for what he had done to Dad, but that he adored Grandma. She told Dad one day that after Stan caused all the trouble they were never 'together' again; she meant they never slept together again bless her!"

"So was your Dad OK with Stan after he apologised?"

"Yeah I think he was but the whole thing really rocked his world. I think that was a big part of his decision to join the Army. Yes he needed a better wage with us three kids but I'm sure he want to get us all away from Stan. But once Dad got going in the Army Stan was very proud of Dad's fast promotions and medals and told everyone he could about his high achieving step son."

"But what about you though, how did you feel when your Mum told you?"

"Well at first I was gobsmacked of course and had no idea Stan had been such a bastard. Then later, when I was on my own... well things started to make sense..."

"How do you mean?" I asked.

"Well it was just a feeling I'd had and still have to some extent today, just a feeling that I'm not sure where I belong or where my roots are. Of course I'm English on my passport but I've always felt that... I don't know... just felt kind of different and... I don't know... it's hard to explain..."

I nodded and could see this was really a big thing for her.

"So did you ever try and find out about your real Grandfather?"

"Yeah I did once, when I was in my early twenties. I talked to Grandma and also her sister because they were always really close so I knew Grandma would have told her lots about the guy she'd met. Grandma didn't really want to talk to me about it but I knew she sort of felt like I did, that there was something about that man and that was why we were so close. Maybe I looked a lot like him..."

She paused to finish her coffee. I stayed quiet.

"When she did mention him her eyes kind of lit up and looked sad at the same time if that makes sense; I could tell she really wished she could have stayed with him and still felt something for him after all that time and only one night together.

"Did you think of going to Italy to try and track him down?"

"No, I couldn't have afforded it. I did teach myself Italian though and found it came really easy. Maybe I will go there... one day... and find him myself..."

As we finished our coffee I sat back in my chair and wondered what else was to come from this woman's story. Already a huge event had rocked her and her family, especially her dad, to the core, something which changed him forever. I took a deep breath and turned to a fresh page in my notebook. We had only just begun and I could not wait for our next meeting.

CHILDHOOD

"So let's go back to when you were five and your Dad joined the Army," I said as I sipped my coffee.

It was a few days later and we were back in my flat. I got the sense that Marie was getting more relaxed; today she'd turned up faded old Levi's a chambray shirt and a kind of biker's jacket. She looked good in anything. She sipped her coffee and then nodded, resting the cup on her thigh.

"OK. So of course I don't remember this from the time, but Dad joined the Army as a Private in The Royal Regiment of Fusiliers. This is, or was, I know the Army's always changing, an infantry battalion with over 600 men. Their families would be stationed with them if they were married. Grandma Alice's sister Florence had seven kids, the oldest being our Tommy, who had joined the Fusiliers a short while before Dad. As well as being cousins they were good mates too. They knocked around Bolton together when they growing up so obviously later on Tommy told Dad how good life was in the

Army. So we were shipped off to Colchester, my Dad's first posting after training."

"What do you remember about going there? Did you really understand?" I asked and she laughed.

"I remember thinking we were just going somewhere for a holiday so I didn't understand why everything had to be put in boxes! Not much else really except making sure my toys got packed."

"Mum still talks about how dad had said we have a married quarter in Colchester and the march in is such a date. She actually thought we had to march into the house! We still laugh about that"

"So what was it like when you got there?"

"Small! We lived in a tiny married quarters at 92 Humber Drive and there was a coal fire in the front room with a curtain that blocked off the bottom of the stairs..."

She laughed again and finished her coffee.

"I do remember that all the bloody furniture was Army green! Can you imagine a young wife today that's use to Laura Ashely or Ikea putting up with that!

"Anyway, I remember a real sense of having a larger family than I already had. There were always other Army wives or couples in our house and we were always going round to theirs. That made it brilliant for us kids; loads of parties and stuff always going on in the barracks. I know a bit later I realised there really was such a strong sense of 'family' and our bonding with all the others was very obvious."

"What about school? Was there a special one for you Army kids?"

"No there wasn't. I went to St. Martin's which was just one of the local Primary School, but most of the kids there were us pad brats."

"Pad brats?" I asked, puzzled, "where does that come from?"

She laughed and shook her head.

"I can't believe that still came out automatically after all this time! Sorry... Any area where there are married and family quarters is just known as the pad and therefore soldiers' kids, pad brats."

"What's your biggest memory of that school?"

"Nits!" she said and grinned. "I got my first head full of nits off some Vietnamese kids who were refugees. My Mum still tells that story about how my hair was down to my waist and just full of bugs. She came into school in a right strop and marched me straight into the Head's office and threatened them with all sorts if they didn't get rid of these Vietnamese kids! Even being quite young I remember I was really embarrassed and that was more about my Mum than having bloody nits!"

"I got some once" I told her, "and my Dad wanted to cut all my hair off! I had really long hair like you and I remember my mother carrying me down the street with my Dad running after her with the scissors!"

"Oh God that's hilarious!" she said, "even worse than mine!"

I put aside my own memories to focus on hers.

"Do you remember what happened to the Vietnamese kids?"

"Oh they stayed of course! Actually they were really nice kids and we were all fascinated that they didn't speak much English. We sort of looked after them."

"Were you happy then?"

"Yeah I was. I liked school but I can't remember any of my friends' names at all and definitely not my teachers' names."

"Was your Dad around at this time or was he posted somewhere?"

"Well this was the early 70's and the troubles in Northern Ireland were at their most ferocious I guess. Dad was away a lot, either training for Ireland or actually on the streets there. Us three kids didn't really understand the reasons behind why he had to go there every so many months, it was just accepted that he did and Mum was always there for us."

"Do you remember how she was, your Mum? Was she OK or sad or what?"

"My Mum has always been a relatively sad person. Later on she did have other wives as friends, but was never really close to any of them and I think she resented the close bonds some groups of wives had together. She kept her distance a lot, but I guess she was OK and when our Dads were away we were always in and out of each other's houses for a brew or whatever."

"So what are your biggest memories of Colchester?"

She paused for moment and then I saw a grin start to form. For one second she looked like the child she was remembering.

"The bloody dog! We were asked to look after a gorgeous Lassie type of dog for one of Dad's higher ranking Senior NCO's, probably a Sergeant Major or something like that, while he was away. Our garden had a 6ft fence that backed onto a row of garages, but this bloody dog actually managed to jump over that fence and we lost it! Dad must have been really embarrassed telling this guy!

"I remember it was very normal on the patch to see the lads in the regiment training for Northern Ireland. They all had weapons and would crouch at the corner of a house watching. They would speak into their radios then after a while get up and carry on walking slowly to the next crouch point." As she relayed this it seemed so normal to her. For me I can't imagine in my hometown anything other than the number 19 bus trundling along our road! What an exciting childhood!

Marie burst out laughing and said "mum always says she made gravy under gun fire in Colchester, meaning these exercises around the patch................hilarious."

"Then there was one Christmas I really remember. First of all me and my brother sneaked all the chocolates off the Xmas tree and hid all the foil wrappers in our sister's toys so she'd get the blame, even though she was too young to have done it! Then they both came to wake me up on Christmas morning dead excited and my brother told me I should go and see what I'd got! They had opened *all* of my presents and the rest of the family's as well. It's still a big family joke now."

"Any bad memories?"

"Well, my Dad was shot while on one of the battalion tours of Ireland in Belfast! I clearly remember the housing warden knocking on our door to tell my Mum and her breaking down and a neighbour coming in. Turns out he was shot in the bloody hand! But still it was a big shock."

"So your Mum was just told he'd been shot but they didn't say how bad it was?" I asked incredulously. Marie was telling me this shocking event like it was just part of everyday stuff! I was truly amazed at this.

She shook her head and I guessed it was still a bed memory in some ways.

"I vividly remember this Sergeant coming next and our Helen was hanging onto Mum's leg as this guy was telling Mum to not worry, but Dad had been wounded in Ireland and was in the local civilian hospital. I was worried for Mum as she was really upset, but honestly I didn't understand what it all meant. I remember the neighbour sending us kids upstairs but we crept down again and listened behind that curtain at the bottom; but we were still none the wiser."

"How was your Dad when he got home?" I asked next and she laughed once more.

"Oh he was fine! He came home from Ireland to recover and bought his first car with the compensation; he got a silver Ford Escort. It was great running all over the place in that car, us three kids fighting in the back 'cos we were squashed and Mum and Dad shouting at us! As soon as he recovered he got sent back to bloody Ireland!

"He told me a couple of years ago that when he was first taken to hospital to have the wound dressed the nurse that was supposed to treat him refused to do so because my Dad is Catholic! So bad were the troubles then that he was left for hours while they found someone who would even speak to him.

"The only other, what you might call bad memory was when our Andrew went missing; he must have only been about 4 years old. They had helicopters out and all sorts and after six hours or so he walked in the house like nothing had happened! He'd been up to a vast area called Friday Woods with his friend Simon. Dad was so relieved he smacked Andy and put him to bed. I've never seen my Dad hit any of us ever apart from that one time."

"So how long were you there for, in Colchester?"

"About four years I suppose. Dad got his first promotion from Private to Lance Corporal and the battalion got their next posting to Fallingbostel in West Germany at around the same time. We were all really excited and even Mum had never left the UK before I don't think."

She paused to have a drink of water and then laughed.

"Mum took us all out to Ipswich to get new clothes because she said 'God knows what we can get in that Germany!' Then she was cleaning and scrubbing everything in sight in the house for days because when you 'march out' of married quarters in the Army it has to be spotless or else your hubby risks the embarrassment of a charge! The house smelled of ammonia and polish for weeks before the leaving day finally arrived and we went to Harwich to get the ferry to Hamburg."

"How did Germany compare to Colchester then?"

"Oh it was exciting at first but I guess I was getting older and a bit more aware of things."

She paused and I waited for her to gather her thoughts.

"I guess it was time of mixed emotions."

"Why's that then?" I questioned.

"Well the worst part was because Dad, along with many of the other guys, turned into a right drinker. The bars in the town survived on the squaddies spending their money in them so they were always full of our Dad's!"

"Was he just drinking beer in the evenings and getting drunk or was it worse? Like whisky and drinking it when he got up?"

"Only beer. His usual routine was getting up for work, not drinking during the day at all but going straight from work with all the other guys in the platoon he was in and drinking beer until the early hours of the next morning; this was probably 4 or 5 nights a week. But he never missed a day's work and he was never in trouble in the Army—ever. In fact he was awarded the Long Service Good Conduct Medal in his 17th year in the battalion."

"So his behaviour was actually typical then?"

"Well yeah. In Germany it was a well-known fact that all the guys drank; it was a given on any posting to Germany, almost as if it was expected of them. I know we'll come to this later and I've told you bits of this before in Bali, but when I was 21 and married to my first hubby, a Scottish soldier, we were posted to Berlin and it was one of the worst times of my life because of this culture of drinking."

She was right, I did know some of things about her first husband and it wasn't good. I left it for now but made a note in my book about her and Germany; I could sense that the whole memory was still pretty raw. I went back to her father.

"I know you said he never got in trouble or anything, but was he really OK for work every day?"

"I know what you mean, but he's just one of those people, lucky bastard, who has never had a hangover in his life! So yeah he was able to carry out his duties as a soldier without any problems. I've actually got in touch with many of his colleagues in the battalion on Facebook and he was well respected…" she paused and then added more quietly, "shame it wasn't the case at home."

"Why's that? What were the issues at home?"

"In Fally, as we used to call it, was where I began to pick up on my Dad's aggression. Since I've got older I've wondered if this was PTSD—post traumatic stress disorder—from Northern Ireland or even earlier with the revelation about his Italian father. Stan and his revelations with regards to my Dad's Italian heritage must have effected him somehow don't you think? Whatever caused his aggressive nature it's still with him now. I clearly remember my brother trying to pull my drunken Dad off Mum one night, Andy crying and shouting for him to get off her. Dad had started when he got in from the pub because his food wasn't on the table."

"Was he actually hitting her often? How did you feel about that?"

"Yeah, he was violent with Mum quite often, but she told us kids to keep out of it. We were her number one priority and all she ever tried to do was protect us from it. The trouble with Dad is that he bottles things up and then explodes; us kids hated this aspect of our lives. Funnily enough though it didn't overshadow our time in Germany and I think that's because Mum held it together and carried on as normally as she could. She never seemed any more depressed than normal and I guess she must have become very good at acting like she was a happy Mum and hiding it from us kids. I'm sure when we were in bed she would cry."

"You said that after he hit Andrew in Colchester he never hit any of you kids—so was this really was the case?"

She nodded her head, uncrossed her legs and sat forward; a clear sign how serious all this was.

"Yes absolutely that was the case. He has never been violent with us. He struggles to ever show any love or emotion or how he's proud of us, but to this day never violent... Mum must have had enough one time though. She got us all wrapped up as it was winter and the snow was high on the ground and she marched us to a phone on the side of one of the blocks of Army flats; these phones were for the families to get through to the Military Police or the Families Office. I remember her crying and begging the Families Officer for tickets home to the UK. We never left but I often wonder what happened after that. It was never talked about and as I said, Dad never got in trouble.

"But did her doing that make him stop being so violent?"

She shook her head.

"It was always swings and roundabouts with their arguments and him being violent; he'd have good patches then bad. I bet all that happened after that night my Mum tried for all of us to leave was him being pulled in by his Sergeant Major and be told to rein his wife in because she was making waves for him! That's how it was in the Army."

"Mixed emotions means there were some good times though..."

"Oh God yes! Many of my childhood memories of Germany were of proper winters, with snow higher than the cars and huge Easter eggs done the German way. Oh! And the horse! Every year a German fun fair used to come to Fallingbostel. It used to be situated not far from the patch on a farmers wasteland. They had lovely horses so us Brats used to go and feed them with stolen carrots from the farmers crops. One of them took a liking to me and got the most ginormous hard on and started chasing me across this field! I remember all the other kids killing themselves laughing and it was funny but god that scared me off horses for life! We had Military

Schools where all of the kids were pad brats and we had to travel to these schools in rickety old army surplus buses. I remember really yummy spicy ketchup and the youth club in the barracks.............It was at Gloucester School in Hohne in Germany I met who was to become my oldest friend, Shelly................" she remembered fondly.

Now she laughed and relaxed back into her chair again.

"Germany's where I started getting feelings of fancying boys and even young soldiers; so many really good memories of Fally. Every month the German households got rid of their rubbish by leaving it out on the street for the dump truck to pick up. I remember our Andy going out rummaging one day in all this stuff and for some reason he brought home a wedding dress; knee length and all white lace. It was lovely, but the silly bugger went and put it on we were all in fits of giggles... it was so nice to see Mum actually laughing."

"Was your Dad always in Germany then?"

"On no, they still had to do Northern Ireland tours and exercises all over the world. He was in Canada once and sent us all a present; I got a Red Indian doll, Andy got a tank or something and Helen got a massive speedy Gonzales toy. I can't remember what Mum got, but one of the lads dropped this big black bag off for us and it was like a second Christmas."

"You mentioned Army flats before; so no houses in Fally?"

"No, we lived in a 3 bed flat in a block of 4 which backed onto a dark wooded area. In that wood were wild hogs and we used to hear them at night. I shared a bedroom with Helen which was awful. She was so messy and dirty and I was the opposite.

Everything had a place on my half of the room. I said about boys a minute ago and from our bedroom window I could see where my first crush lived—Chris. I loved him but he never knew! He was a real ruffian, always in trouble at school but I didn't care. I used to while the night away just staring up at his window in case he looked out at mine... bugger never did! My friends were Shelly, Debra, Katie and Julie and we knocked around together a lot, but I was painfully shy at school... painfully. I never spoke to anyone other than my close circle. Infact Shelly and I were the shyest in our group and we were just 2 peas in a pod. She lived in a different town as her dad was R.E.M.E, Royal Electrical Mechanical Engineers to you love!" she laughed.

Of course, based on our time together so far, I was very surprised at this revelation of shyness.

"Really! Do you know why you were shy?"

Another shake of the head.

"No... I just was; still am really. I actually asked my brother and sister this question some years ago and Andy said he didn't know, but interestingly Helen said it was because I was overshadowed by her and Andy all the time because they got on more than me and Andy or me and her."

"But to just come away from your childhood for minute, you say you are still shy now?"

"Yeah I am in certain circumstances. If you'd not been such a prat and fallen over my handbag and had just sat at the bar instead I'd probably kept my head stuck in my iPad. What I've done over the years is to use my feminine wiles a lot to overcome it. Or like that night in Bali and me and my bloody vibrator, I over compensate by being brash sometimes and my friends now say I'm hilariously funny too. All of that stems from not wanting to be the shy mute I was growing up!"

I stayed silent to let her just carry on where she wanted to go to next. She laughed.

"I started my periods at 12 and thought I was *so* grown up! I remember that it was just before one of the times Grandma Alice and Stan came to visit and I couldn't wait to tell her. On one of their other visits Mum and Dad had took them to the Corporals' mess for an afternoon 'session'. Brandy and peppermint drinks were on tap for Grandma and she got very drunk! When they all got home late in the afternoon she fell into a radiator in the hallway of our flat and hurt her head. She was shouting about not letting her grandchildren see her like that and we were all in hysterics!"

"Despite being shy then you were just a normal teenager?"

"Oh sure. That same visit we took them to a huge NAAFI in one of the other camps and I was just starting to take notice of music. It was the late 70's and I loved anything electronic especially Gary Numan and Tubeway Army. I was looking at their album and Stan asked me about them and I rabbited for ages about how brilliant they were; he bought me the album but I think it was to shut me up! I've still got that album; I love music and still listen to all the electronic 80's bands. Still go to gigs when I can."

"How was your Dad's relationship with Stan during these visits? We're they OK together?"

"A bit staged I guess you might call it. Dad was always pleasant to him for Grandma's sake, but if Stan was around he would usually just busy himself with fixing one of our bikes or cooking dinner or whatever. He obviously grew to be quite an expert at this since we never knew a thing until I was 15. We never felt an atmosphere and we loved Stan and their visits."

"So if Chris the ruffian never bothered with you, what about other boys if you were almost a teenager?"

"Well I was starting to get attention and I suppose in today's world it would be looked on in horror, but I had my first sexual experience around that time. I had started babysitting for Mum and Dad's friends when they were out together and one Saturday night a 17 year old Squaddie from my Dad's battalion was babysitting next door. He'd got his kids to sleep and then come to visit me; Steve his name was. We would cuddle a lot and then I'd pretend to sleep and he'd touch me a bit. I just thought it was exciting since my hormones were running riot from my getting attention from what I saw as a grown up squaddie! My friends were dead jealous!"

"You pretended to be asleep?" I asked with a grin, remembering an experience of my own that I was *not* going to repeat. She laughed and for the first time I noticed a hint of that shyness she said she still had.

"Oh God yeah! Thing was I had no idea what was going on, with both me and him and also because I was so shy. I had no idea what I was supposed to do so I just shut my eyes and enjoyed it! Anyway, Steve got posted away and a bit after that I had my first proper date with a boy, another soldier's son but not in Dad's battalion. I can't remember his name for the life of me but Dad drove me to the pictures and this boy paid for me to see Grease; Mum had bought me a special outfit. After the Steve episodes I must have been old before my time sexually and I expected at least a bloody snog but got nothing. He didn't touch even my hand and I cried in the toilets because I thought he didn't like me!"

We had to stop here and get some lunch because I was laughing too much and I needed to change the tape. Once we'd settled down at the dining table with a salad we carried on. She went back to some of the not so good times.

"A bit after that Dad had got this really big Austin Princess car and we went on a road trip with his friend Jock and his family and we drove all the way down to Rimini in Italy for 2 weeks. It was a great holiday apart from Mum being really physically sick a lot of the time and having to stay in bed. Although us kids were worried about this both mum and dad made sure we had the best time here. I remember I had a lovely red strapless jumpsuit that I paraded around in. I had big boobs even then at just 13 and though I was shy I loved all the attention from those Italians! Later on when I knew my roots it seemed like I understood why that holiday was so special."

She stopped to eat some more of her food then, her face more serious again, she carried on.

"Shortly after this trip Mum ended up in hospital. As well as her problems with Dad and his drinking and the violence, Mum actually hadn't been well for a while and it turned out she had a huge stomach ulcer; Dad can't have helped. She looked like a ghost now with almost transparent skin and she was so thin. Anyway, it turned out the ulcer had burst and she was gravely ill. Dad took us to visit her one night in the Military Hospital and the nurse asked me to help her change a bag of fluid; it was awful. I was so shocked at this person who almost didn't look like my Mum lying in this bed, sedated after having had half of her stomach removed. I couldn't speak and I remember even Dad crying…" she brushed away a small tear and then gave me a wry smile: "She recovered, in time and he returned to drinking- normal life for us."

"What's your biggest memory of time in Germany? Have you given me that already?" She shook her head and looked the most serious I had ever seen her.

"During my school days in West Germany, inevitably our history classes taught us about the two World Wars and of course why us Pad Brats were in Germany as families of serving UK soldiers. We didn't live far from Bergen Belsen, the notorious Nazi Concentration Camp. One day a bus load of us British kids went on a field trip as part of our history class to this place and I will *never* forget that day as long as I live. I was about 11 years old, painfully shy and quiet and had to take all the upset of what I saw inside me and on my own.

"First of all there is a small museum with a map of the camp and lots of pictures of the Nazis standing around in groups laughing and smiling. Those first pictures actually looked quite normal but then the horror started that will always be in my memory. The pictures then started to show the same Nazi soldiers herding these terrified Jews into big pits. These pieces of history that have been captured on photographs were just compelling to us kids and we were all very quiet for the rest of the day.

"I remember turning a corner in this weird little museum, which every visitor has to walk through to enter the camp itself, and found small television monitors with actual footage of these appalling atrocities afflicted on the Jewish race. I just couldn't believe my eyes; women and children being separated from their husbands and fathers by these Nazis, pulling them by their hair. The women and children were then kicked to the ground only to be spat on and stripped of their clothing. The children were screaming and their mothers were trying to protect them as their men watched on unable to do anything to help them. Then I watched in horror as a bulldozer just scooped them up and tipped them into a huge pit. The Nazis then aimed their machine guns on them as they fought for their lives in that pit and the Nazis were laughing. Some of the women and kids were clearly still alive as the soldiers started to bulldoze earth on top of them, burying some of them alive."

She stopped at this point for a moment and pushed away her uneaten food.

"A lot of us were really crying at this point and our teacher was just very quiet as he led us out of that building; he was in tears himself. Outside, it was sunny and calm, but I remember two boys in our class being sick in the bins. Purple heather grows on the mounds that were once these mass graves of Jews. Nobody knows where this heather came from. No one has ever planted it. It's now a beautiful memorial to those who were persecuted and killed here. As we were led around that place of death we were struck by the silence and a guide told us that no birds sing there at all. In fact there were no rabbits or moles or any wildlife............... at all..."

"Do you think it was wrong to show all that to you kids?" I asked, shocked at what she'd been exposed to. More and more I realized just how normal my childhood was compared to hers.

"Absolutely not! It's why the British Army are still posted to Germany now and I know that military kids are hard enough to see this stuff. I have a friend who really wants to go and visit Belsen. I have told him what happened when I visited but it's not putting him off. I think everyone should know what this place is like and what happened there during the war. It's such an important place as are the other concentration camps."

"You have your own kids now of course. When they were 11 would you have wanted them to see it?"

"Actually, no. My girls haven't had the military background I had. I don't know how they would react to this if they saw it but strangely I'm glad I did"

"Is that it for Germany then?"

"Yeah I guess so.................such a fantastic place to grow up" she said with a sigh and then smiled:

"Next stop Palace Barracks, Holywood, County Down, Northern Ireland and we were all shitting ourselves! The troubles were still raging on and the streets of Belfast were not safe for our Dads and us Pad Brats either."

"That sounds like it's going to be fun" I said starting to clear the table. Marie got up to give me a hand; I knew she had to be leaving to get back to the restaurant.

"Oh there's a *lot* to come for NI" she said with a grin, "wait till you hear about my exploits with the randy Private on the NAAFI steps!"

"Oh come on what's that?" I asked, putting the plates back on the table.

"Oh no you'll have to wait for that one, but I will tell you this..."

"What?" I asked in anticipation.
"It's bloody funny!"

GROWING UP

Marie was thirteen when the family arrived in Palace barracks in Northern Ireland. Although a new posting was always exciting, she had had to say goodbye to Shelly which was really hard. However in an Infantry regiment you travel with hundreds of other families that have been there the whole time wherever the posting was. Growing up with the same kids was familiarity and this made everything feel safe and secure somehow.

Built within the grounds of former stately home, it was close to the small town of Holywood and a little bit further away was Bangor with its rugged coastline and the beautiful tourist attraction Giants Causeway. In the opposite direction was the City of Belfast, where all those years ago Marie's dad had been shot by the IRA.

"But it's not like bloody Hollywood in America is it!" Marie said to her friends Debra and Katie after their first day at Holywood High School. The girls were sitting in the kitchen in Katie's house; everything here was green just like Colchester and Fally, thought Marie. Katie laughed:

"My kid brother heard we were coming here and the daft bugger thought we were going to America. So I told him Dad had got a part in a film as a soldier and was going to famous!"

Marie said that she'd planned telling her brother Andy the same thing but he wasn't that daft. The family moved into a married quarter on the edge of the camp next to a massive sports field. Everyone very quickly found out where all their mates were housed within the Barrack walls and started going out, hanging around the NAAFI among other places. Being a smaller area than Fallingbostel, and being teens now Marie and her mates would make a point of going outside the camp on some made up errand just to walk past the guard room and the sanghas (sentry boxes) placed on the road opposite to ogle at the young squaddies on stag. They could fill full days with this activity Marie recalled laughing. Her dad would have killed her if he knew!

Life in Northern Ireland was surrounded by security issues and the children were told not to speak outside of camp whilst on their own for fear that they would be targeted as pad brats. Going shopping was a nightmare for the family as the car had to be checked with a mirror on a stick underneath the chassis for any bombs that may have been planted. Once in Belfast, shopping meant navigation around all the high corrugated iron barricades all around the shopping centre that and having bags checked to get in. Every member of the family had a pass to get in and out of camp.

Soon it was time for the July Orange marches and Marie and all her friends were confined to barracks. These volatile events, where Unionists would march en-masse through Republican areas with bands and flags, would usually incite riots and trouble. The police and Army were out in force, but all of the families had to stay on Palace Barracks. Marie thought it was all crap felt more cooped up than ever.

Holywood High School was OK, but Marie couldn't really complain. She'd passed her 11 plus exam when she was in Germany and had the option of going to the local private school. She was all for the idea because it sounded 'dead posh' but when she got there to meet the Headmistress her world almost came to an end.

"Well we'd love to have Marie here of course," said the snotty cow; Marie's description, "but all that hair would have to go. We do have rules here you know."

Marie glanced at her Mum in panic; she'd just got it to the point where could sit on it and there was *no way* she was getting it cut. Marie could tell her Mum wasn't happy either.

"Are you suggesting we don't wash her hair?" her Mum asked from the other side of the huge old oak desk.

"Oh no, of course not" replied the Headmistress, a little flustered and Marie grinned; her mother kicked her under the desk. "It's just that we like all our girls to have nice and neat short hair; it looks so much smarter when the girls represent the school. I'm sure you understand Mrs Turner."

Marie wanted to say that 'no she didn't understand' but she'd only get kicked again. Her mother said they'd think about it and when they got back to the car she told her mother that there was no way she ever wanted to set foot in that place again. Her mother tried to persuade her but Marie only got angry and upset; Holywood High School it was then.

On top of the move to a different country again, there were other changes going on in the Turner household when it came to schooling. Marie's brother Andrew heard about a boarding school in the Lake District; he just 'had to go'. This was a school for the children of people serving in the Air Force and Navy as well as the Army and places were subsidised by the respective service. Marie was also offered a place, but with her severe shyness, she turned that down as well. Her sister Helen actually went there for a while, but she ended up coming home as she was homesick. This return was much to Marie's consternation, on the basis that the two girls had to share a room again.

By now, as well as being 13 going on 14 and wanting her own space, Marie was fastidiously tidy whilst Helen, to use Marie's words, was a 'slob' and Helen's side of the room, as described by Grandma Alice, was a midden! This led to a room of two-halves and endless arguments which their mother either chose to resolve or ignore. During the latter months of living in Fally and getting ready to move to Belfast, Marie's shyness reflected in her spending a lot of time on her own away from her family members.

She would sit for hours in her room listening to BFBS radio and just being quiet and getting lost in her music. She had a keyboard by now, one of the many Christmas and birthday presents they all got every year. She adored listening to a new song she liked and then learning the tune by ear and just playing along. In retrospect she often wondered if she had a musical talent and why she never pursued it.

The point was that Marie just loved her own company and was getting a bit jaded with her brothers quips about her nose amongst other things; these things always seems worse to teenagers Grandma Alice told her one day just before they left Germany. Marie was glad when Andy went away but she was also getting increasingly despondent about her Dad's treatment of and aggression towards her Mum. There was also the fact that she had started to notice that her brother and sister got on a lot better with each other than she did with either of them. Marie considered this sense of isolation and she decided that, quite simply, she felt different to all the rest of her family. She tried to rationalise it to herself and couldn't; she was just 'different' and always felt like she didn't belong to this family.

It was three weeks into her new school she experienced the first of her problems in Northern Ireland; this one was not of her own doing. Every day at school meant another day coping with being extremely shy and reserved; she'd just put her head down and tried to remain inconspicuous. However, this unfortunately becomes like a magnet for bullies and she had caught the eye of one particular Irish girl, Andrea Mooney, who really took a dislike to Marie. The reason for this dislike was never really fathomed out, other than perhaps the girl was a Catholic, but there wasn't usually problems between the different religions in a school setting; she was just a nasty piece of work.

One Wednesday morning, as Marie and her new classmates were getting changed for gym, the teachers were called out to deal with twisted ankle. Marie was sitting quietly in the corner, tying the laces of her trainers, when she sensed someone appear next to her. She looked up and there was Andrea Mooney with two of her cronies behind her. She tried not to look up but a strong finger was placed beneath her chin. Her eyes briefly met the other girl's before she looked down again.

"I don't like you Turner" sneered Andrea in harsh accent.

Marie ignored her and just hoped she would say her piece and go away. That or the teacher would come back.

"I'm talking to you bitch!" was the next comment; this was also ignored.

"Are you listening to me you English bitch?"

Again Marie said nothing and this was too much. Andrea dropped her finger from Marie's chin and quickly and violently grabbed a handful of Marie's polo shirt scratching her ear and face as she did so. Two buttons flew in different directions as Marie stumbled to her feet; and made her big mistake. She tried to free her shirt from the other girl's hand and in doing so, Andrea stumbled backwards and had to be stopped from falling by her two friends. As she regained her balance her eyes narrowed and she launched herself at Marie.

"You feckin' English bitch!" she screamed then she punched Marie hard in the mouth. Marie stumbled and tripped on her untied laces and was instantly in a heap on the floor. That was when the first kick caught her on the thigh to be followed by one in her stomach. The air shot out of her and she immediately started retching as she naturally tried to curl up in a ball. Now totally terrified, more than she had ever been in her life, she was too late to protect her head as another kick landed on her ear.

In the background she heard Andrea's friends telling her it was enough; but Andrea disagreed and she now jumped onto Marie's body and began the worst of her damage. With her extremely dirty fingernails she began to claw and scratch like a wild cat at Marie's face; the result was two weeks off school for Marie as she developed a terrible case of impetigo. Twice a day her Dad had to try and clean the terrible infection in her face and right ear as waves of nausea and faintness would wash over Marie and she would have to sit down on the loo until it passed. When she got back to school Andrea was made to apologise to her; in later life, Marie would always say that was her first taste of knowing when someone is not exactly meaning what they say and faking it.

But life wasn't all that bad and it was a few months later that her Dad, who had been on foot patrol in and around Belfast for a week, came home with a surprise. He was smelly and tired, but seemed happier than when he normally came back from weeks of patrolling in and around Armagh and Marie noticed something moving in his combat jacket pocket. It was March, close to her birthday and Marie was sure that this was something to do with it. After Marie and her Mum and sister harassed him for about five minutes to tell them what it was, he reached into his jacket and produced the most adorable and tiny Springer Spaniel puppy. She was tiny, brown and white and just perfect.

"Say hello to the new addition to the family!" he said and Marie screamed in delight, sending the poor dog back into the jacket. To Marie she was just adorable and thoroughly gorgeous. Having never had a dog since the Lassie dog debacle in Colchester, the family now had another member and Marie couldn't have been happier.

Soon earning the name Pincher on the basis that she was always trying to pinch people's slippers, the dog had been found by her Dad's platoon when on foot patrol around some farmland near Belfast. They had come across a farmer killing a number of pups. Michael offered to take the last one alive, the runt and he brought her home with him. She as destined to be with the family for 15 years.

After everyone in the family household had really settled into the new routine of Pincher being there but Andrew being away at school, the second bad thing happened. This one was Marie's doing and it wasn't just one incident, in fact there were several but the last was by far the worst. Now 14, she was babysitting a lot having already gained experience in Fally and she would look after younger kids on a Saturday night whilst the parents went out to Sergeants Mess do's. It was during this period that Marie started taking things. She really didn't know why she did this and still doesn't know today, but it got worse; much worse.

First of all the things she took were a book or a pen, but then, one night at the start of the school summer holiday, she went babysitting for her Mum and Dad's best friends. She had just got the children off to sleep and she came out of their bedroom onto the landing; the door to the children's parents' room stood invitingly open and she couldn't resist the idea of a nosy around. She looked in the mother's wardrobe, but her clothes were a bit boring and then she went over to the dressing table. Standing in the middle was a jewellery box, just like one her Grandma used to have, and Marie settled herself on the stool to go through everything. Most of it, like the clothes, was unexciting then, tucked away in a small box, she found two gold rings. Without a second thought she slipped them into her jeans pocket.

All was quiet for around five days and Marie kept the rings in her room in a pair of socks and whenever Helen wasn't around, just sat and looked at them and felt exceptionally guilty; she also felt helpless to do anything about it. Then all hell broke loose. Marie was in the kitchen making a cup of tea when her Dad came home early; she overheard him tell her Mum that the Regimental Sgt Major had pulled him in because there was an accusation of theft against Marie. She was rooted to the spot and didn't know what to do, but would later say she would always remember the look of utter disappointment on her Dad's face when he and her Mum came into the kitchen.

"Where are the rings Marie?" he asked quietly; he only really ever raised his voice to her Mum and that was when he was drunk.

"What rings?" she replied, knowing the guilt would be written all over her face.

"The rings you took from Jeff and Fiona last Saturday night when you were babysitting..." he just left it there.

"I never took any rings!" she retorted, her voice rising in pitch with her growing panic.

"Oh come on Marie. Apart from Fiona you're the only one who could, I hate to think you would, go into her jewellery box." Now her father was getting a little louder, frustration and anger being added to his disappointment.

Marie had the look of a cornered fox as she kept glancing over her Dad's shoulder to see if she could make it out of the room; her Dad took a step to one side and her exit route was blocked.

"I didn't take any bloody rings alright!"

And so it went, with Marie now being accused by her mother and sister as well as her father until after a period of silence, his voice just became very quiet again.

"It's OK, just give us the rings and it will be forgotten" he said.

"I... did... not... take... anything!" Marie shouted and finally she pushed past them all and ran upstairs. Feeling so terribly guilty, both for taking the rings in the first place and for lying so blatantly to her family, what she did next was equally stupid, if not more so; she recovered the rings from her room only to go to a window at the back of the house and throw them out into the garden. In total panic, the only thought she could get straight in her head was to think that if she get rid of them then nobody would know they were there.

She'd got as far as lying on her bed, her face stuffed in her pillow, when all three of them came in again and the accusations started up once more. Later on Marie would liken it to some police state interrogation; but it worked. Eventually she broke down and admitted to what she had done. She had never cried so much in her life and felt terrible for embarrassing her whole family, but she was made to join her Mum, Dad and sister, on their hands and knees in the garden, searching for the rings. They were never found and she discovered later that they were Fiona's dead mother's rings and were deemed irreplaceable; Marie really hated herself and regrets to this day what she did. She never stole anything again.

Her punishment was to be sent away, to be apart from her friends, for the whole of the holidays. Her Dad dealt with it the only way he thought would protect her and he sent her to stay with

Grandma Alice, which in fact could have been seen as no punishment at all. But her Dad thought it was for the best for Marie, to protect her from a small enclosed camp with a battalion of gossiping wives and spiteful mothers. However, all Marie could see was that she had been banished from everyone close to her, away from her friends, until it blew over. At the time she hated her Dad for what he made her do and felt that he had dealt with it really badly. Later she would wonder what else he could have done and realised that she was one very confused teenager.

So she spent 6 weeks with Grandma Alice and Stan and simply loved it! She soon got over her initial resentment of being sent there and would while away the days making jewellery with wire and beads and chatting away to her Grandma like nothing had happened. Having already been exposed to Marie's love of music in Fally, Stan would tease her about not being able to watch Top of the Pops on Thursday evenings; the real highlight of her week. Marie would settle herself in front of the TV and demand total silence so she could watch the likes Gary Numan or Human League or Orchestral Manoeuvres in The Dark. She had to grumpily explain to Stan that this was what OMD stood for and not, as he teased her, 'orrible music done badly! There were The Human League,The Cure, Japan, Duran Duran and Spandau Ballet to be marvelled at never mind the gorgeous Dave Gahan of Depeche Mode! Marie totally immersed herself in the electronic and New Romantic music of the times and when back in Belfast, she still loved to play the album Stan had bought her a couple of years before in Germany. She always thought at the time that her destiny was something to do with music, although alas it was not to be.

As much as Grandma Alice and Stan recognised that Marie was growing up, there were still times during Marie's stay with them that suggested they still thought of her as 'their little grandchild'. The house was a typical northern back to back terrace and still only had an outside toilet. Marie was too embarrassed with the idea of having a chamber pot beneath her bed and insisted she didn't need it; Alice had different ideas. Every night during her six week 'exile', Marie was woken up by her Grandma in the middle of the night to go out to have a wee in the cold air... in case she wet the bed!

To add to Marie's love of the latest 80's music, a major influence on how her life would start to change when back in Bolton was made her cousin Samantha, who was a year older Marie. Sam started taking Marie to the local youth club and introduced the younger girl to a world she knew nothing of! She had been brought up in barracks and military schools and this was suddenly so much fun. Here Marie started to properly dance to the music she loved and found that she loved it. She just got lost in the music, forgot about all the other kids there and just danced. After that Top of The Pops meant dance practice as well and Stan used to tease Marie that she had a bad arm since she only used one of them when she danced.

The Royal wedding for Charles and Diana took place when Marie was back in Bolton and she watched this with Sam and her mother, Auntie Angela, along with Stan and Grandma Alice. Stan was much amused in the fact that Marie and Sam had 'dressed up' for the wedding, both wearing their pedal pushers and frilly New Romantic shirts;

Grandma Alice said they looked lovely. Marie was transfixed by Diana and she was very fortunate to meet the Princess later in her life, something she will never forget as long as she lives.

So her punishment turned into a period of time she would always remember with great fondness. It was the end of the summer holidays and her exile in Lancashire came to an end; it was time to return to Northern Ireland and Palace Barracks and school! Having built up a picture in her mind that she would be ostracised from everyone, she was dreading it. On the last evening, before she would get the coach back to Belfast, she broke down when she was talking to Grandma Alice.

"But no one will ever want to speak to me ever again!" she wailed, as tears poured down her cheeks.

Alice tried to stem the downpour with a tissue.

"I don't think you'll find it as bad as that Marie love" she said, pushing her favourite granddaughter's long dark hair away from her face.

"When I spoke to your Dad about what time you'll be back he said that things had been sorted."

"Yeah! Sorted as in probably getting sent away again to that prison school where our Andy is!" she said, wiping her nose with another tissue.

"It's not a prison Marie and you know it. Andrew's very happy there and that's not what your Dad meant."

"Well what did he mean then? Am I going to be banned from going out with my friends or something...?"

Marie didn't say what the 'something' might be and Alice didn't bother to ask, she was sure that her son would do the right thing and recognised that Marie had been punished enough. As if to prove that point, Marie's tears got worse again.

"Oh Grandma! I'm just so sorry for what I did and I feel guilty all the time. I just can't believe I was so stupid and I'm so embarrassed as well cos everyone will think I'm some kind of freak!"

Alice took Marie's hands in hers and made her look into the old woman's eyes.

"Marie my love, you're a wonderful young girl that did something very wrong but you've paid your penance as your Dad saw fit and it's time to move on. Your Dad knows that too and your Mum will as well and so will that Jeff and Fiona. Now just stop this worrying and I'm sure that when you get back everything will be OK and you'll get your life back to normal."

And that was exactly what happened and all Marie's worries and fears turned out to be totally unfounded. Her Dad met her at the coach station and all he talked about was to ask what she'd been doing and to tell her all about Pinchers latest exploits. Neither he nor her Mum ever mentioned the rings again other than to tell her that Fiona and Jeff had been extremely forgiving and gracious and had kept the whole incident a secret to save everyone in the Turner family from further embarrassment. At the time and still now, Marie was eternally grateful that she actually found everything to be the same as when she left. All her friends had missed her, but obviously didn't know anything.

So she settled back into school for what was her exam year and now her sense of feeling nervous related to doing well academically. There was a lot of expectation from her parents, as the eldest of the 3, as well as her teachers, all of whom said she was extremely capable. Marie did work hard but this was also the time when, after her experiences in the civvy youth club with her cousin, she started to come out of her shyness a little and boys started to feature in her life. Around the time she turned 15 she had her first proper boyfriend, whose nickname was Sticky; she never did find out his real name. He was quite dark looking and had long hair and they would climb the hill at the back of the barracks and sit at the top together in silence. They kissed occasionally, but nothing more and the relationship didn't last too long.

As the time to revise got closer, her hormones began to take over as Marie, as Grandma Alice would describe it, really blossomed out into a young woman. She was very much starting to attract attention, not only from the boys in her school, but also from the young squaddies in the battalion too. At 15 years old it seemed such a grown up thing to Marie to have an 18 year old soldier fancying her!

One of them in her Dad's platoon took a real shine to her. He bought her the Human League album 'Dare' and wrapped it up in a box and put it on top of their dust bin for her to find. Marie was very impressed but her Dad felt the opposite and she never heard from the young soldier again. However, that album started her life-long love of Human League and one night shortly after she got the album, she and Katie went to the Kings Hall in Belfast to see them in concert. They went without anyone knowing because it was a very dangerous thing to do and during the whole evening they didn't open their mouths at all in case someone realised they were English. For Marie it was so exciting and she still goes to see them now whenever she can.

All of the attention from boys and men was now starting to be at the centre of her life and she found that she didn't really care about the exams anymore. By that time she was almost becoming a fixture at the youth club on the camp as she started to lose her shyness even more. She started to get a bit of a following as a 'rude girl' as she danced on her own to anything Ska from the 2 Tone record label, but especially to all her electronic favourites. The other kids used to line the walls to watch her dance to Toyah's 'It's a Mystery' and Japan's 'Quiet Life'; she was the centre of attention and she loved it.

With her New Romantic clothes and her crimped hair, at last Marie was starting to feel comfortable with who she was. The attention she was getting now was not like that she'd received from Andrea Mooney and she managed to get large periods of time away from her family's constant bickering and shouting and mickey taking about her appearance, nose, whatever they could really. She really felt as if she was in heaven and loved her life as a 'noticed' 15 year old living on a military barracks full of testosterone!

FIRST LOVE

Making her mark on the youth club and continuing to make impressions around the barracks was helping with Marie's shyness. As her friends were starting to get together with boys who were the sons of other soldiers, Marie was setting her sights higher; she wanted to bag herself a soldier. Of course there were plenty to choose from and they all would no doubt have wanted to be picked. By now Marie's figure was that of a full grown woman and she could only have been described as a head-turner; well that's what Grandma Alice's latest term for her was and she was proven correct many times a day as Marie went to and from school and then hung around the barracks at night. Standing outside the youth club to be 'seen' was as big a part as being inside dancing and it was on such a night that Marie and Steve first saw each other.

Steve was a young squaddie, not long turned 19 and he'd been in the army for 6 months. He was tall, with dirty blonde hair with a long fringe that he kept flicking back with a cheeky jerk of his head.

He had lovely honey coloured skin. Later on they would talk about each other's striking looks being one of the things that first attracted them to each other; but that was only one because there were so many. The night was a surprisingly warm one. Marie was wearing a dress that she'd found which looked like one she'd seen Toyah wearing, but her eyes were heavily made up like Siouxsie Sioux. Steve was still in his uniform, but heading back to the block on the barracks that was single soldiers living accommodation, having just come off patrol. He ambled over to her and the group she was with and her stomach fluttered.

"You look like a bloody Banshee!" he teased and she managed a shy grin, knowing it was a compliment. "Nice dress though" he added and she felt her cheeks redden beneath the heavy make-up.

"You into Siouxsie then?" he asked and she nodded. She wanted to speak but was afraid her voice would squeak.

"You do talk I suppose?" he asked and she nodded; this time she did stay silent on purpose and then couldn't help but grin and he laughed. The sound made her stomach churn again; it was a deep and throaty laugh and just so sexy.

"Alright then" he said, seeming to ignore her friends, some of whom were giggling at what was going on. Marie just knew they were jealous. "Here's a question you can't nod your head to, what are you doing tomorrow night?" His Lancashire accent was as strong as hers still was and she loved it.

"Going out with you?" she asked, having no idea how she could ever have been so bold. She heard her friends gasp behind and he looked really taken aback. Then he gave her the grin that she fell in love with.

"Tomorrow night then Marie, I'll meet you at the end of your street at 7."

Of course she wondered how he already knew her name, but later found out that he'd been asking about her and had come by the youth club on purpose in case she was there.

"Righto then, err...?"

"Steve. See ya."

And with that he was gone; and so was Marie. The next 24 hours could not go fast enough for her and she was ready an hour before she needed to leave the house. Her Dad was on duty, but her Mum sensed something was going on.

"What's up wi' you then?" her Mum teased.

"Nowt Mum" she answered too quickly wishing her mum would pay her no attention.

"Really? You don't look like there's nowt going on love!"

"Just going to the youth club, alright Mum!" she snapped and her Mum laughed, before adding as she left the room.

"Well you have a nice time love" she said knowingly and Marie blushed as she realised it was at last time to go.

On that first night, her and Steve just talked and talked and Marie felt it was like they had known each other for years, but had spent some time apart and were now just catching up on news. They found a spot to sit on the NAAFI steps that would become their special place, for all sorts of reasons, and very quickly they became inseparable. Marie was supposed to be revising for exams and she did do some studying on the nights Steve was on duty, but when he was free she was out of the house like a shot. Her Dad soon got to know she was seeing him of course, but he was OK with things as long as she was home by 9pm.

Once back in her room, Marie would feel like she was glowing, such was that intense feeling of first love. She looked like a woman on the outside, but inside she was still a girl and the whirlwind of emotions she was feeling seemed to engulf her so much it sometimes felt as if she could not breathe. Apart from her relationship with Grandma Alice, she had never really experienced unconditional love before and knowing that Steve felt just like she did heightened the sensations she was feeling. She had seen 'love' on the TV and in the movies, but as far as she was concerned those portrayals showed nothing of the truth. What she and Steve had was so completely opposite to her parents it seemed and they were still together; that meant that her and Steve could only ever go on for ever and ever.

Her time with Steve was naturally helping with her confidence and when she did go out, but he wasn't around, she started drinking. Whereas before she had refused, she soon became one of the instigators of a drinking session and one of those led to the night of the broken tooth. Marie and her friends were sitting behind the cookhouse with some vodka she had pinched from home and they had some fizzy limeade to help it down. That particular night she got very drunk and decided she wanted to see Steve who was on duty at the side gate to the barracks. She zig-zagged her away across the camp, luckily without being seen and there he was, resplendent in his uniform and looking, as far as Marie was concerned, so very handsome.

She managed to get herself let out of the main gate on the basis that the guys knew who her Dad was and they watched her weave her way over to Steve. When she was less than six feet from him she tripped and smashed her face on the curb. She was so drunk she didn't actually feel anything at the time, but did tell him later that she clearly remembered part of a tooth going one way and her dignity the other! His off-duty friends managed to sneak her back to the house, but the next day her parents were horrified. As she went off to the dentist she was told she was grounded for a month. She remembers Steve being allowed to come round to the house though- maybe Mum said to Dad he was being too strict not allowing her to see Steve.

But a week later her Dad relented and her and Steve were back on the NAAFI steps and it was here, on that night back together, that the relationship got a lot more serious. They had chosen the spot because it was quite secluded, with only an occasional patrol, and their early kissing had progressed to Steve had spending a lot of time inside her bra. He always said her tits were gorgeous, but that night his hand wandered lower for the first time and soon found its way between her legs and inside her panties. Marie had never experienced anything like it and her hand now just naturally reached out for him and she fumbled to unfasten his jeans. Eventually she felt his hot hardness in her hand and that was it, there was only one thing to do.

"Oh God I want to fuck you Marie" he Mumbled, as her hand worked harder.

"Well, what's stopping you?" she said breathlessly, before adding, "the bloody patrol will be here soon!"

Steve laid her on the bottom step and quickly pulled off her panties before pushing his jeans and pants down to his ankles; then he moved in between her legs. At first it was a bit painful, but that was soon forgotten as his thrusting got stronger and stronger. Marie couldn't believe how amazing it felt to have him so close and so deep inside her and as she saw the moonlight shining on his bare arse she began to have her first ever orgasm.

She was so proud of having lost her virginity that she told her friends at school the next day and they didn't approve. However, Marie couldn't stop smiling all day and after that they were like proverbial rabbits and made love whenever they could. Marie always said she never had sex with Steve; they only ever made love to each other and that feeling still lasts to this day. But Marie's love making was without any experience and so she would just lie there like the proverbial sack o' spuds while Steve did his thing, always in that traditional missionary position. She never knew about any others, but always had an orgasm with him; something she'd only achieve a few times with any other man after that.

Most of their coupling was done on the NAAFI steps in between patrols, but there were a few times they managed to do it in Marie's house, with the family downstairs. The first time they were alone though this happened, Marie made him stay downstairs whilst she 'got ready'. This was to be the first time they could take their clothes off properly and Marie stripped off as quickly as she could and dived under the covers. She shouted him to come up and it was only after he had pulled back the covers to stare at her naked body that she realised she was still wearing her little white socks. As he reached for her he said nothing, but later on he told her that he thought it was incredibly sexy.

Marie felt that there was no way on earth she could be any happier, but then the problems started when she realized that her period, which had always been intermittent, was terribly late. They had only ever used a withdrawal method for contraception and not long after she turned 16 Marie realised she was pregnant. For a while she didn't tell anyone, but eventually made an appointment with her doctor and went alone; when he confirmed her worst fears not even the thought of being with Steve could lift how bad she felt. She had just left school and had a job washing up in a hotel kitchen; the day she went to the doctors she walked out without telling anyone and was almost fired the next day.

She'd had many sleepless nights and her Mum and Dad both sensed something was wrong. So had Steve, but she still hadn't told him yet. The day her situation was confirmed he was out on patrol in Belfast and she could not get hold of him; there were no mobile phones in those days. Instead she took a long walk on her own until she got home and had summoned the strength from somewhere to tell her Mum and Dad.

Her Dad was just silent and her Mum started crying and nervously watching her husband for his reaction. Neither asked them how Marie was feeling. When her Dad finally spoke he just said:

"You are such a disappointment to me Marie. Don't even think about keeping it!"

And that was it. He left the room and didn't speak to her again for five days. Her Mum made it clear that *she* wanted to keep the baby and bring it up as one of her own which of course was out of the question in Dads eyes. Marie was just mute and had enough on her plate without all the drama.

Steve called that night as scheduled and she told him the news. Immediately he asked how she was and how she was feeling about it, but Marie didn't get chance to discuss anything because her Dad took the phone off her and sent her to her room. Behind the closed door she could hear her Dad downstairs, ranting at Steve and she heard her Dad say to him that he would 'see him' when he came back off duty. : Poor Steve. Here he was patrolling the dangerous streets of Belfast having been told by his very young girlfriend that she was pregnant only to be told by her father that he would be 'seen' when he got back to camp. He must have been shitting a brick!

Marie never found out what happened at that meeting, but a few days later her and Steve were back to seeing each every night they could. She knew that either Steve had stood up to her Dad, but agreed to the termination or her Dad had told Steve that if he agreed to the termination he could carry on seeing her.

So her Dad arranged for them to go and see the Army doctor to get permission to get the termination. They were in his office for a long time and the doctor seemed to remain unconvinced that this was the outcome Marie wanted, but she was just numb and was going along with her Dad's decision; he really handled everything and that was fine by Marie! Despite her now being 16, Marie was allowed no say in the matter and a termination was organised in London.

Marie was 16 weeks pregnant when all this happened and after the doctor consented she went off to London with her Mum; there was no chance of a termination in Northern Ireland at that time. As Marie left the house she wished she could be going on her own like she had when sent to stay with Grandma Alice; her Mum was totally over dressed in a long leather coat and leather boots looking like she had come out of the set of Dallas and to top all that she was crying like it was *her* that had to go through everything.

Once they arrived at the private hospital, Marie was given her own room because she was so young and so far gone- this was an actual baby not simply a foetus anymore. She still had her long hair and cried for the first time since she had left the doctor's in Belfast when a nurse shouted at her to get her hair under the green hat ready for surgery; that's when she got scared. She'd never had surgery before, but she wasn't even thinking that at the end of it she wouldn't have a baby inside her anymore. All she could think about was how Steve was going to finish with her now, no thought of the baby inside her that would die that day, after all 16 is no age to be dealing with this. These overpowering thoughts and this overriding anguish were that of someone who really, was still only a child. She was as upset about being apart from Steve more than she was about losing the baby; maybe even more. That was her naivety.

When she came round her Mum was in the room and, in no surprise to Marie, was crying again. Marie just felt terribly empty and all she wanted her mother to do was to piss off and leave her alone. There was a telephone ringing in the room and still in her somewhat sleepy state she answered it. The woman on the other end of the line clearly thought that she was talking to Marie's Mum because she promptly passed on the message that the baby had been a boy; now Marie cried like she never had before and this time it wasn't about Steve. Looking back she feels that at that very moment she grew up a little bit.

Once she got back to the barracks she was relieved to find that Steve felt no differently about her, in fact his feelings seemed to have deepened and he did two things; he arranged to take her home on leave to meet his family and he asked her to marry him as soon as they could. Nothing that had happened with the baby had changed how much they loved each other and the baby was never discussed. Marie never learnt how he felt about it all, about his thoughts when her Dad had 'ordered the termination' with no regard at all for the father's wishes or hers.

Today, with the benefit of hindsight, Marie knows that it was the right thing to do and that it would have been madness to go through with the pregnancy; neither she nor Steve was in a position to give the child a proper upbringing. She knows her life would have been so different had she given birth to that baby boy, a little boy she never named. For this she will be forever grateful to her Dad.

But it wasn't long afterwards that it was time for her and Steve to part. They were both equally devastated. Her Dad got a promotion and with it came a posting away from the Battalion to Warminster and Steve, and the rest of her Dad's unit was posted to West Berlin. After her move, but before his departure for Germany, Steve visited her in Warminster for a weekend. She met him off the train and she was filled with excitement at seeing him but also total devastation that in 2 days she would be saying goodbye. Her Dad wasn't supposed to know, but he saw them on the High Street on that Saturday afternoon. They ducked into a shop doorway and Marie was terrified, but later that night when she went home her Dad never said a word. She guessed that he knew Steve would be leaving for Berlin the very next day so wasn't going to upset her any more than she already was.

So the last time she ever saw him was that Sunday in 1982, when she had to say goodbye as he caught the 2.30pm train. She truly felt as if her heart was being ripped out and she stood sobbing and waving goodbye long after the train had disappeared from sight. She had never known heartbreak but this was definitely it and it was all consuming. A few people stopped to ask if she was ok but she couldn't even speak such was this pain she was feeling. Steve called the house phone every night for a few weeks from West Berlin and they made plans for when he would get some leave and come home, but their young lives moved on and they drifted apart; Marie was now attracting attention in the new camp, The School of Infantry, Warminster. The hot pain of heartbreak had subsided and she didn't want to be dishonest. One night when he called she took the bull by the horns and they agreed that the distance was not good for their relationship. She was so distraught at losing him but was very grown up about it and relished being free to explore other opportunities! However she never forgot Steve and through the years wondered what had happened to him and his cheeky grin.

The whole episode with the baby was devastating, especially for her mum and had taught Marie a lot, but as much as it seemed at the time that being apart from Steve was almost worse, the whole affair was traumatic and heart breaking and she still often thinks of that baby boy today. But she also knows that her Dad's decision and her going through everything made her stronger in many ways. A few years ago she actually thanked her Dad for being strong and making that heart-breaking decision for his daughter, but she knows her Mum sees things differently. Apparently she had begged her husband that Marie be allowed to keep the baby and her Mum would help bring it up. When she spoke to her Dad about it he asked her if she regretted not standing up to him and she reassured him that he had done the right thing for her. He said that it's something he doesn't regret but that he's had to live with all those years.

MEETING JACK

Once she'd finished telling me the story of Steve and the baby, Marie had cried quietly to herself and I left her alone as I went to get some more coffee. We were in her house, but I was used to where things were after a number of sessions to cover her time in Belfast. Eventually she wandered in and gave me an apologetic smile as I handed her the mug of coffee.

"Oh ta," she said with a final sniff and grin, "you must think me a right soft bugger!"

"Far from it" I told her, "first loves never go away and those with 'added complications' like yours are always going to rake up old emotions."

She went over to sit at the old pine table and looked into her coffee. The tape machine was in her living room, but I was happy just to chat.

"I still think of him from time to time" she said quietly, "even without you raking up old memories!"

"So what happened to him?" I asked, joining her at the table. She laughed ironically.

"I heard through the grapevine that within 2 months of my finishing things he married a girl from his home town. My sister always said he did that on the rebound; I guess she's probably right...

"Their marriage didn't last long apparently and he's had children with others. I suppose I'd like to think I'm thought of by him now and again too, at least to remember the innocent virgin he swept off her feet!"

She laughed now and seemed to have got over the upset.

"I can still remember so vividly his arse in the moonlight! I told him later they could probably have seen the bloody thing from outer space!"

"There was one time I was with a guy in some woods" I told her, "I'd be about 18 at the time, and he was just about to start fucking me when a bee stung him between the cheeks of his arse!"

Marie spluttered her coffee all over the table and I had to grab some kitchen towel to wipe it.

"Oh bloody 'ell Tina! You mean he was running round screaming blue murder whilst you were lying there with your legs apart waiting to de-flowered?"

"Well I'd already lost that but yeah he did; silly bugger wasn't looking where he was dancing around and cut his foot on some wood!"

As I left her with tears of laughter this time, I felt she'd be OK again to carry on and I went to fetch the tape machine. Once we'd got a coffee re-fill we began recording again.

"So how was living in a new camp in Warminster without Steve?" I asked.

"Pants! It was a new place and a different way of living as the married quarter was on the patch out-side of the camp, a bit like Colchester I suppose only we didn't know a soul here and I missed him like... well I mean I *really* missed him. I was dead anxious about what he was doing without me."

"Did he call you?"

"Yeah; every night at first, but then those calls reduced to every other night and then dropped away to once a week etc. He was always very loving on the phone, telling me he missed me and couldn't wait to see me on his leave, but that wasn't enough for me..."

"So what happened?"

"My eyes started bloody wandering that's what! I knew I was in love with Steve, but I was a 16 year old living with soldiers everywhere and I was a new face on camp... I was getting *lots* of attention! So I ended it with Steve. He was heartbroken and so was I but even at 16 I knew it wouldn't last with the distance between us."

"Life moved on then?"

"Well yeah; life moved on... and I got a really great position with a promise of a start of a career!"

"So you didn't go back to school after Belfast?"

"No. I'd had enough. My Dad was the Signals Colour Sergeant and was responsible for the Communications Centre which included the Army Telephone Exchange and he got me a job there. All the people working there were civilians, a small team of 6 women all working in shifts so that the exchange was manned 24/7. Dad heard of a position there and bagged me an interview. My claim to fame is that at 16 I became the youngest Civil Servant in the country!"

"Were you happy doing that? How did you get on?"

"I absolutely loved that job. I was trained on the old plug board system and never knew what I could be dealing with from one day to the next or even one call to the next. We had to deal with connecting military calls from all over the world to various parts of the School of Infantry; from the Brigadier to Private Bloggs in the Guard Room. All of my colleagues were older than me, 4 of them near retiring age. I didn't care and I loved them all since they mothered me of course."

She finished her coffee and as she rinsed the mugs in the sink she started chuckling to herself at a memory.

"I soon got started on night shifts" she said as she sat down again. "Shit they were scary at first, being almost alone in the exchange and I would be locked in case of some terrorist attack. The theory was that if anyone attacked the camp the exchange would be safe and therefore it would be able to contact the outside world. The only other person on a night shift was a serving member of WRAC and she was responsible for monitoring for any Sitreps—situation reports—coming in on huge machines like a big printer. But she was in another part of the old building and it was creepy! I got used to it and as the girls got to know me we used to have a chat and a brew together to while away the hours in my exchange room. Sometimes when it was quiet we'd listen to the latest music or even order in a Chinese!"

"What were things like at home?" I asked.

"Things did get slightly better when we were first there. Dad was enjoying this posting and Mum was 'allowed to work' so was meeting new friends. I was working and when I was on night shift I was sleeping all next day so hardly saw anyone at home. My brother was still enjoying boarding school and my sister was at a local school so it was 'settled' for a while.

"It's funny looking back you know Tina, but there were still no demonstrations of love at home. I honestly didn't know that this wasn't a normal relationship between parents and family until I made a new friend. All my old friends were in West Berlin with the battalion but I became good friends with a girl called Gemma who lived 3 doors away. She went off to Yeovil to nurse training quite soon after I got to know her, but I remember being in her house one day and needing the loo. She told me her Mum and Dad was in the bath together so I couldn't go!

"Now this was a complete revelation to me at 16! I mean I actually didn't know that parents do that sort of thing because my parents didn't even talk to each other unless they were arguing, never mind be loving in front of us kids. I couldn't stop thinking about that! Her parents in a bath together! I was very confused because that just wasn't my normal sphere of life!"

"Dad really enjoyed this posting. He took mum to loads of Mess do's and even invited some Private soldiers home for Xmas dinner one year. This is something that Senior Nco's do with lads that are stuck on camp for the festive period. The constant piss taking in front of these 2 lads at the Xmas table was relentless with dad and my brother pissing themselves at the fact that dad had put Alka Seltzer on the table as a condiment. He asked the guys not to stare at mums hands too much as the scars are from where she drags her hands on the floor when she walks! Then there was the '2 slices of gravy or 3' one! It was banter to them but I'm sure mum was really upset in the kitchen. And still the verbal blows kept coming from Dad and Andy with reference to my nose or my sisters weight. She had always been what they termed as chubby. They even thought of a name for her- Chuberella or Chubster. Just awful." She said with anger.

"So how long was it after you split up from Steve before you had a bloke in your life? You said in Bali that you met your first husband in Warminster."

"Yeah I did but that was after being there a while, but he was still the first person I went out with properly as such but... oh bloody hell Tina I've just got to tell you about the officer!"

"Sounds intriguing! So what's that all about?" I said, intrigued.

"Well... on the exchange I was a new voice and got talking to loads of guys and after about six months one of them, an officer, took a particular fancy to me and arranged a visit to the exchange on the pretence of researching possible placements for cadets. Anyway, he invited me to lunch and egged on by my workmates, who were all older women than me of course I said yes. Even my Dad had encouraged me by telling me I could do worse than an officer! The thing is though that there was no food and lunch consisted of a drive into the gorgeous Wiltshire countryside."

"So what happened?" I asked knowing that this was going to be good.

"Well he parked up the car in some dead quite place and turned to me... oh he had this horrible greasy black hair and was not even good looking! Well anyway, at first he was still the gentlemanly officer and he chatted about my school days and about what good soldier my Dad was. I actually thought I'd met a soldier that didn't want to just grope me but have a conversation. Then he started...

'Do you want to sit a bit closer to me?' he asked with a strange look in his eye that made me think he looked like some kind of alien; I really didn't know why I'd said yes to his invite..."

By now I was starting to recognize Marie's' constant changes in body language. Now she was extremely animated, throwing her hair back, eyes bright, before leaning in closer to stamp meaning on this tale.

"'Suppose so', I replied and with that he started on my tits! Well I was a big girl already by then and he fumbled my shirt open and stuck both his hands into each side of my bra. Once he'd managed to pop both of my tits out his eyes most definitely had a look of an alien!"

She shuddered and laughed at the same time as she poured us both a glass of white wine; it was near lunch time. She took a drink and then put her glass on the table.

"Well he held one in each hand, as if he was choosing bloody at Safeways and hardly even blinked. Anyway, cos I had to look away from his alien eyes I looked down at his trousers and saw that there was a bloody great cucumber on the shopping list as well!

'Oh God, here we go again' I thought to myself and then the bugger got hungry! He leant forward and after a few tentative licks of my nipples, which I actually thought felt quit nice, he opened his mouth wide like he was on the fucking dentist's chair and began pushing my tits together!"

She grabbed again for the tissue to wipe her eyes and then continued; by now I had tears coming to me eyes as well. She certainly knew how to tell a story!

"So having got my nipples as close together as he could then entered the afternoon's main event, the tit eating contest, with the prize going to the guy who can get the most breast in his mouth as fast as possible! Oh God Tina, I wasn't a virgin after my time with Steve, but what he was doing was gross! He forced me into the corner of the car and I swear to you, as he slobbered all over my chest and I decided that if he'd gone for sucking one at a time rather than both at once, as big as they were, he might have swallowed it completely and I'd have been up on a murder charge for mammary asphyxiation!"

By now we were both helpless and I was unable to speak for laughing so much and then she continued with the story.

"Well finally I'd had enough and I told him that they would still be there tomorrow and said did he know that Friday's the eat all you can for a fiver night!

'But darling' he said in this bloody plumy voice as he finally sat back but still staring at them 'those breasts are just magnificent". 'Yeah and you're an arsehole' I thought as I tucked them back into my bra and fastened my blouse, still shuddering at the thought of him slobbering like a demented dog. So then I turned to him and asked sweetly if we could go please because I had to get back to work. Wanker asked me out again a few times but I always told him I was busy."

We just had to take a break at that point and chatted as Marie made us some Ceaser salad for lunch. Once we'd sat down again at the kitchen table I put a new tape into the machine. I was overwhelmed by this woman's story. So far she had only told me her history to 16 years of age and already had been through so much.

"So tell me about when you met your husband. Jack right?"

"OK then; yeah I guess it's time for the infamous Jack. Well now, every day I had to walk past the guard room and it seemed that each time there was always this dark haired Scottish soldier waiting. He never said anything, just smiled; he was quite a bit older than me. Anyway, one hot sunny day, a little while after my 18th birthday, he finally spoke to me asked if I would like a piggy back to work! I said 'oh yeah right' assuming of course that he was joking; but oh no. He threw his glengarry, his army cap off and chased me! If he' been seen by a higher rank he would have been jailed for sure, but I just floated to work that day.

"So I started seeing him and learnt that he was 10 years older than me and married to a girl called Annie who lived in Scotland with their daughter Mary. Actually, that wasn't an issue to me and I didn't feel guilty or anything because he told me they were separated, which in actual fact was true. I knew that for someone like me he was quite a catch. He was the Provost Corporal, which meant he looked after all soldiers that had been charged with various misdemeanours and he had a bit of a name for himself as the 'beast master'. The Provost staff 'beasted' the prisoners each day and they would do stuff like make the prisoners march around the camp carrying huge cannon shells up above their heads, or clean up the camp picking litter and so on. It was all about humiliation and this boosted his ego no end! I guess that should have been a warning sign; that and him being an alcoholic too. But I was very young and naive and I missed all these signs in the early months of our relationship. We were having sex all the time since he had a room in a block on camp to himself and it was our pad, but it was never home really."

"Did your Dad know what was going on?" I asked and she shook her head, pushing her empty plate to one side.

"One night there was a Corporals' mess versus Sergeants' mess games night, which was men only and Jack planned to tell Dad at this event. Well Dad came in at 3am and woke me up and sat me down in the kitchen for 2 hours interrogation! He'd of course been drinking and went on and on about how disappointed he was that I was with a married man with a kid. That I could do so much better and that my mother would be devastated, but I didn't care since I already saw Jack as my ticket out of there.

"So it was out of the bag and Mum didn't say much really, just asked me when she would get to meet him. A few nights later we bit the bullet and he came round and we all sort of chatted for a while until I couldn't stand it anymore and we went out instead taking Pincher for a long walk around the patch. My Mum was just being twee and my Dad was sitting there grinding his jaw, something he only did when he was angry.

"Anyway, by then it was already 2 years after Dad's posting to Warminster and he was going to re-join his battalion, who were all coming back from West Berlin, in Catterick. You know it never entered my head that Steve was now going to be in the same country as me, I was so wrapped up in my fab job and as well by now in my volatile relationship with an alcoholic..."

Marie looked pensive and I even sensed some regret; there seemed to be only one question to ask:

"After your experiences with what your Dad was like with your Mum didn't you actually want to run a mile from getting into a situation like that yourself?"

Marie laughed wryly and looked more relaxed as if that moment of being in the past was just that again, in the past and she could talk about things dispassionately.

"You know Tina, I've been asked the question so many times why I stayed with Jack, married him and had his children, but I've got no idea. I was so sick of being with my parents and I was just an anxious mess at 18. Anyway, I moved into a flat in Westbury with him and I remember Mum sorting out bedding and stuff for us, I had no clue really what I needed. Jack had got an extension to his time in Warminster, which was probably because his battalion didn't want him back, so I carried on working on the exchange and he was still Provost Corporal."

"So your Mum and Dad and sister moved to Catterick Garrison then?"

"Yeah that's right," she said, before breaking smiling at a new memory. "That's when I got Bo. Pincher had her own pups by a gorgeous black and white spaniel called Lucky. Me and Jack had one of these pups and I called him Bo. When Pincher was giving birth it was hilarious, like bloody 101 Dalmatians! When each pup was born it went round the camp like wild fire! They were all claimed even before they were born and it was big news because Dad used to take Pincher everywhere with him so she was really famous on camp. We have a set of lovely photos somewhere of her sat at dads desk with his beret on"

She smiled a little more at the memories of the dog and then grew serious again.

"Anyway, it was after they'd gone that I had to grow up fast. Dealing with an alcoholic at that age was awful. It was gut wrenching and at times it even felt like a slow suicide. I lost all of the confidence I had built up as a teen in Northern Ireland."

She looked wistful again as if back once more in the past and I gave her a break as I made some coffee. Marie got up and cleared the table, putting things into her dishwasher.

"You OK?" I asked as I poured the coffee.

"Yeah I'm fine, hon" she said as she got us some milk from the fridge before we both sat down again.

"So it was a kind of love-hate relationship then?" I asked and she laughed out loud.

"Oh God no Tina, love didn't enter into it! No, no I never considered myself to be in love with Jack at all. I was *in love* 2 years previously with Steve; that was love..."

She shook her head at the memories and sipped some coffee, her eyes distant over the top of the mug. Then she smiled as she put her drink back on the table.

"So here's a sample of life with Jack in those early days. During our time in Warminster he was arrested three times by the Military Police for various misdemeanours, like taking petrol from the Army Land Rovers for his own car and being drunk on duty and so on; stupid bugger was jailed in his own camp Guard Room with the people he was supposed to looking after! He also gave me crabs. Can you believe that? Bloody Crabs! I was so downbeat I just accepted what he told me, that he'd caught them from the beds in the jail whilst sleeping; what an idiot I was!"

"So was he drunk all the time?" I asked and she shook her head.

"Actually no, he was a binge drinker and at times he had weeks if not months where he was sober which were good and life could be OK, but I was always waiting for that next binge"

"So tell me some more about him then" I suggested.

"You know, it was during one of his sober periods he told me about his life. He was one of 6 kids, the second youngest of five boys and a girl; Catholics from Glasgow. His Mum died when he was 6 years old and he told me he remembered her dying in hospital. The priest was by her bed and the family had been called for; his Mum's sister took all the kids in to see her. Once they were all around the bed his Dad walked in with his 'fancy piece' who already had his Mum's fur coat on!"

"Nice man" I said and she nodded her head as she took a drink.

"Apparently his father stayed in the room until his Mum was dead and then just walked out, abandoning all the kids. They were brought up by various members of the family and Jack ended up with the Aunt who'd taken the kids to see their mother. He told me he loved her and she did her best, but they had nothing; as a teen he started drinking. He never spoke to his father again after that day in the hospital and, maybe without a man in his life, he was troubled to say the least."

"What about his wife, Annie I think you said and his daughter?"

"Oh he hardly spoke about them and he never paid a penny in maintenance either. He got his divorce from Annie when I was 19 and he got posted to Colchester to be back with his Battalion. I was devastated to leave my job at the exchange and the older women tried to talk me out of going with him. I said I had to and my supervisor tried to get me a posting to the switchboard in Colchester, but it was all military personnel so it was a no go. I was gutted.

"When we got there we stayed with some of his friends and their wives in their married quarters at first until they got sick of it; well sick of Jack being pissed all the time. We had to leave and got a room in a house living with a couple who were mentally ill; God that was awful. Jack went off on duty every day and I tried to find work, but more and more I was becoming like my childlike self again. I was introverted and anxious all of the time and Jack, now back with his old buddies in the Battalion, started not coming home at night. He would stay on camp drinking for days and I just felt very angry, isolated and lonely...but stupid me still stayed."

"What about your parents? Did you have any contact with them in those days?"

"You remember I told you about my Dad's cousin Tommy who first encouraged him to join the Army?" I nodded and Marie carried on. "Well Tommy was also posted to Colchester and unbeknownst to me Dad had asked Tommy to come and visit me at my digs to find out how I was doing and where I was living. He turned up one Saturday morning with his wife and I could tell straight away that he wasn't happy. I'd made my room as nice as I could, but there was the mentally ill couple in the living room, letting slip that Jack had not been there for 4 days, it was too much and so embarrassing!

"They said nothing and wished me well, saying that if I needed anything I was to call them, but I knew Uncle Tommy was less than impressed. Later that day Dad called me and went mad, telling me I needed to go straight to Catterick. But for me, that was almost like a frying pan into the fire and still I stayed with Jack. It was around this time he got his divorce from Annie and one day when I he was sober, so I knew he was serious, he proposed to me and like a bloody idiot I accepted!

"I vividly remember calling Mum and Dad to tell them and Dad went absolutely berserk down the phone, the worst he'd ever been, calling me all sorts of names, idiot, moron etc. The lump in throat was so big I couldn't speak and I was so upset. He just didn't realize that if he'd been nice and caring then I'd probably have done as he said; instead he was just pushing me more towards Jack..."

It was at that moment that my phone rang and I stopped the tape and took the call in her lounge, giving her a few moments to compose herself. When I got back to the kitchen she'd cleared away the coffee mugs and was looking out of the kitchen window. She turned around and gave me what I'd come to learn was her 'I'm OK' look and so I just smiled and sat back down at the table and made a few notes about her latest revelations. Eventually she came and sat down and gave me a nod to carry on.

"So the wedding went ahead I guess" I said as I re-started the tape, "but did your parents come?"

"Yeah Dad relented and we arranged to get married on August 1st, 1982 in Richmond, near Catterick. There was my family and that was it; I was

20 years old and didn't have any friends and none of Jack's friends came. Dad had organised the Regimental Colonel's car to pick us up and take us to the Registry Office. In the back of that beautiful car he said one thing to me in the whole 35 minute journey: "It's not too late you know" and that was it. I didn't even answer him. I was an anxious mess and not because it was getting married, but because I was dreading it if Jack got pissed. He did of course and my wedding day was ruined. We had a wedding breakfast in a small hotel that Mum and Dad paid for then went back to their married quarters and had a party. Jack was drunk and had to be put to bed... bastard."

She shook her head at the bitter memory and then gave a small laugh.

"Even though we were now married, my Dad still decreed that we were not to sleep in the same bed under his roof, so for the next week we slept apart in their house! We then had to go back to Colchester and moved into our first married quarters together and I was, as ever, optimistic and hoped for change. So we started married life together in Colchester, in a Battalion full of Scottish people I didn't know but, it seemed to me we had a chance of a new start. How wrong could I be?"

A tear started to trickle from one eye and she hurriedly brushed it away and gave me a weak smile. I knew already that Jack would prove to have been the worst person Marie could ever have met.

"It was only Bo, my loving dog that got me through some of the darkest times in my young life. When Jack was off somewhere getting pissed Bo was my only friend. He was my boy and we were inseparable. I had him until he was 15. He was my life and I still miss him to this day"

Once more, my heart went out to Marie. Her young life had been traumatic by anyone's standards, yet here she was an articulate and stunning lady both inside and out. Whatever was to come, it had shaped her into the woman she is now and felt she was much a 'total woman' than I could ever be. I would never have wanted to trade my simple youth for her torrid times, but I most certainly wished I could be just like her now.

MARRIED LIFE

At 20 years old, Marie was a very young army wife back in Colchester, living within a 600 strong Scottish Infantry regiment. She was one of only a few English wives and kept to herself. Her and Jack moved into their first married quarters on St David's Close. It was a two bed house with a lovely sweet shop bay window at the front, but none of the furniture was theirs; it was the army who provided all that and most of it was green. It hadn't changed from when she was a child.

Jack was on duty a lot, so it was just Marie and Bo, which to her was fine most of the time. But Jack was drinking most of their money and she had to find some work; there was no job on the switchboard this time. She got a job packaging Trivial Pursuit games in a big factory and the money was quite good. They more than needed that when she got the news. She told herself that things would be different now. He will have to change. He will want to change.

"You're what?" he replied when she told him.

Marie smiled as she nodded. She was happy that he was going to be happy—and change.

"Yes. You're going to be a Daddy."

He gave her a huge hug and he was happy. But nothing changed. Things just continued as before. Marie found herself consumed with anxiety once again.

During this time, one of Jack's good friends had married too, and the happy newlyweds moved into the house across the road. Duncan and Jenny's wedding couldn't have been more different to Marie's. Jenny told Marie—at great length—about the lovely lavish family gathering and shared all the photos that documented the big day. Every single one had to be studied just in case someone—like Marie—might think it not possible for such a wonderful wedding to happen. Marie knew it could but not for her.

"And this photo shows the cake from another angle," Jenny said, as she took Marie on the extended tour of her big wedding via the pretty photo album. Everything in order, as a wedding should be, from the big white wedding dress, the three-tiered cake and the huge wedding party. And then Marie had to hear about the honeymoon in a posh hotel in Guernsey.

As Jenny expanded on every detail, even the ones Marie definitely not did want to hear, she thought of her own wedding. There was no white dress, no cake, no lavish reception, no honeymoon and no photo album. Perhaps that was just as well, she thought. It would have only one page, a place for the marriage certificate. You didn't need pages for the no money, no prospects and no fun. It was almost a worthless piece of paper.

So the married and now pregnant Marie was still anxious and living on her nerves. Then they received the news that the battalion was being posted to West Berlin; the Berlin Wall was still up at this time. Marie and the other wives had lots of things to do and despite the huge differences their lives, Marie and Jenny became firm friends. Despite the fact that Marie had been there before, both were excited to be going to West Germany and hoped very much they would be living near each other again.

During this time Jack and Marie went up to Catterick for Christmas because they would be leaving for West Berlin in the following February. In theory it was a chance to say their goodbyes, but Marie's Dad was posted in Cyprus so wasn't there. Marie was not too bothered about that at all, but was upset to find her mother was utterly depressed. It was the worst she had ever seen her. She spent all of her time in bed.

Marie guessed that, with all that had gone on with her Dad, her Mum had probably been suffering depression since they were young. It was a sad indictment that such a situation could be easily explained by all the behaviour in her mother's life. But this Christmas it was particularly bad and her Mum stayed in bed the *whole* week they were there. Marie's brother was also home, but he just brushed off Marie's insistence that their Mum needed help. Her sister was never home, always out with her mates and wasn't much help either.

On one occasion the phone rang and it was Marie's Dad.

"How's things in Cyprus?" she asked, hopeful of even a short conversation with him. He simply muttered that he was fine and asked to speak to her mother.

"I'll just take the phone through to her. She's in bed" said Marie and clearly heard her father's sigh. Perhaps it was understandable that he wasn't in the mood for small talk, but then again he was very much to blame for the situation.

"Right," he said, without asking any questions.

Marie took the phone into her mother's room and closed the door on her way out, but she could hear her sobbing down the phone, saying she had given up and that she couldn't stand it anymore. Her Mum was clearly suicidal, but Marie had no idea what to do about it.

She didn't have an overwhelming natural love for her Mum and felt no burning need to offer any kind of protection; in fact she actually felt that her Mum was being a drama queen again. It wasn't until Marie was in her 40's, the decade when wisdom arrives as an uninvited guest, that someone pointed out that her mother's attention seeking behaviour and playing up was in fact a cry for help.

But that Christmas Marie was still young and she couldn't stand being there. She actually felt a wreck herself. She was pregnant with a continually drunken husband and about to be moving thousands of miles away across Europe. Why was everyone wrapped up in their own world and not paying any attention to her? Had she become such a good liar, she wondered, such a good little actress that nobody noticed her struggles?

They drove back to Colchester early, using Bo as the excuse. Her parents still had Pincher and had kept one of the other pups, Lulu and Bo kept trying to mount his sister. What a family, Marie thought, and smiled for once. Her family now had a case of incestuous dogs!

February soon came around and they travelled to West Germany. Jack had managed to get finance on a brand new estate car and it was full to the brim with their belongings, the dog and them. They arrived at the ferry and Marie was devastated. Bo had to go into a very small kennel for the twenty four hour crossing. He howled the place down and Marie joined him… in the howling.

All the other soldiers and their wives were laughing at her being so upset and not one of them offered any words of comfort at all. Things got worse when it was time to sleep and she discovered that Jack hadn't even booked them a cabin. That would have meant wasting good money and they had to make do with chairs on the main deck, mingled with all the young single squaddies from the battalion.

Marie finally decided she hated him as she struggled to get comfortable chair for a rough 24 hour sea crossing. She was now three months pregnant and was sick all the way while he got pissed in the bar with his mates. She always wondered later, with all the anxiety, that she was perhaps lucky not to miscarry the baby.

They arrived in Hamburg and started their long drive in convoy to West Berlin. When they reached Helmstedt, the start of the 'Corridor', as it was known, where the west crosses the east borders to enable troops to get to West Berlin, she was surprised to see it wasn't actually a corridor or tunnel but open countryside. All the military personnel and their families were given a start time and an end time that they had to report in at in West Berlin. This was so that if anyone went over that time period, it was presumed they had broken down in East Germany or been kidnapped by Eastern forces.

Marie was decidedly nervous; it had never been like that in Germany before. Their car was searched before they left for any documentation or contraband that they could offer to any eastern forces. The military policeman searching them said they could not stop for the dog or for any other reason at all. So they filled up with fuel and set off.

But Marie was pregnant and she needed to pee ... a lot! She knew Bo was desperate and so was she.

"Jack, you'd better stop," Marie said, and Bo whimpered in agreement. It was the middle of the night, pitch black and very quiet.

"You heard what they said. No stopping—not for any reason."

"Well this isn't bloody well any reason. I have to pee. And if you don't stop, you'll have to get used to your precious fucking car smelling like the public lavs!" Now she was speaking a language he understood and pulled into a dark layby, his eyes looking around in the gloom.

"There's probably no one around these parts, anyway. But just hurry up, will you?" The remainder of the convoy continued on ahead without them.

Marie let Bo out and crouched down behind a bush. Any woman will tell you that peeing in the presence of Mother Nature is an exact science. You don't just spout a fountain like a man, in the general direction of a bush or a post or to make writing in the snow. You have to squat carefully, not too low so as to have spiky grass scratching your arse, and not too high so that the flow escapes the intended path and trickles down your legs. Then there is the added complication of how far apart your feet have to be placed so that you don't end up standing in your own steaming puddle.

Marie didn't have time to consider the science, she was desperate, and so her bladder just gushed before she could consider the implications of foot placement or body height. Mid flow, she heard a twig snapping and the next thing she knew she had half a dozen East German soldiers surrounding her with their rifles aimed at her head! Bo was barking at them and one of them kicked him to shut up. He ran whimpering back to the car. Marie managed to get her knickers up and the soldiers had her march back to the car with her hands on her head. When she got there, another two were searching the car and had Jack on the ground, face down.

They put Bo in the car and shut the door on him. Jack showed them the translation card the MP had given them in Helmstedt and they relaxed a little.

"Ja, you haf some drink...?" and a soldier indicated with hand signals that he wanted something to drink and he wasn't talking about water. Jack sighed. Another soldier added his order. "Zigaretten? You haf zigaretten?"

After a short round of negotiations, which also included some cap badges from Jack's uniform that would fetch a good price, we paid the ransom and were released by the now smiling soldiers. As soon as they were back onto the road Jack started.

"For fuck's sake woman! That was ma whiskey and ma bloody fags, too. That kills me giving those up." The car quickly picked up speed, and the faster Jack drove, the angrier he became, swearing and cursing both Marie and the dog as well as the East German soldiers.

“Don’t you bloody well forget that it was me who had fucking rifles pointed at her head!” she cried, but deep down she wasn’t surprised at his uncaring behaviour.

“Well, next time you need to pee, just keep it in. I won’t be pulling off next time you start whining” he retorted.

“I won’t keep it I’ll just piss all over this car and all over you!”

“Fucking idiot” he muttered as felt his pockets for his fags that were no longer there. Marie just started to silently weep, it seemed se was on the verge of tears 24/7 these days. This was not how her life was supposed to turn out.

They arrived at the checkpoint in West Berlin over an hour late. The MP's kept them there and questioned them separately. Jack had told her in no uncertain terms not to tell them what had happened because he would be jailed for sure; engine trouble was to be the excuse. Marie didn't say a word, of course. She wasn’t about to regale tales of having her arse and other bits bared in front of a bunch of soldiers while they watched her try to pull her knickers up once the gushing had stopped. The checkpoint MPs let them get on their way to Brooke Barracks which was to be their home for the next eighteen months. Marie was apprehensive to say the least, but she pushed herself to be optimistic and hoped against all the odds for happier times when she could relax a little. After all, a new baby would ensure that wouldn’t it?

FIRST BORN

They were allocated their new quarters, a two bed upper flat overlooking the barracks and Marie loved it. It was especially bright and spacious, with lovely carpets and a balcony at the back. Best of all was that none of the furniture was green. There was obviously more of a budget in West Berlin!

Marie thought of her childhood that night, and of the time when her Dad was posted to Fallingbostel and there was snow every winter. It was still February and they were in the depths of a German winter that was to last for another month. The flat was cosy, though, and they made it their own. The other five flats in the block housed other battalion families and Marie soon made friends with them, especially Stacey who lived across the landing.

She was also from Colchester and had married Tom two months earlier. Marie thought she was brilliant and they soon began what would grow into a lifelong friendship. Her friend from Colchester, Jenny, now lived some miles away in the other married quarter area. The two friends had hoped to live nearer each other, but they made a point of meeting often.

The period marked a time when life wasn't that bad. Jack seemed settled and happy for once and Marie allowed herself to let her guard down a little and enjoy things. Her belly grew, and she blossomed as a pregnant woman. She had her 21st birthday with no fanfare, no party, no birthday wishes from anyone including her family back home. Just a normal day.

In time, they went to see all the sights in West Berlin—Check Point Charlie, Brandenburg Gate, and the Blue Church. And, of course, the Wall, which divided the Communist East from the West. They would drive to a particular wooded area they grew to like to walk Bo and one day they walked a little further than was usual and reached a quiet area of The Wall. Marie was fascinated by it. Some of the graffiti was fantastic.

Behind the wall was an area designated as no man's land and it was in this area that there were the watch towers of the Communist forces. On that particular day, the soldiers in the watch towers had their binoculars trained on the small party all the time that they were there.

"Jack, what's that?" Marie asked, lowering her voice as though she didn't want the soldiers, who were a great distance away, to hear. Jack saw the red spot Marie had noticed on Bo's shiny black coat and looked up at the nearest tower.

"Shit! They've got Bo in their sights."

Jack continued to watch the tower for a few seconds until Marie had snatched Bo up, protectively cradling him in her arms. Jack motioned back to where they had come from, where they should have remained.

"Let's go!" For once, Marie agreed with her husband, and they left quickly.

Later in life Marie would look back and in some ways marvel at having been posted to Berlin at such a time in history. Surprisingly they were allowed into the East and the soldiers had to wear their number one kit, which consisted of trews, white spats and the Cock Feather in their Glengarry. All the wives loved these trips because everything cost so little there and they never returned empty-handed. It was all cheap rubbish but had to be bought because it was so cheap!

No one missed noticing the stark difference between East and West Berlin. All their cars were out of the 50's, the buildings were all grey and there was no grass. It was as though the entire country was a black and white photo from long ago. The only colour allowed, it seemed, was on the flags that waved from every grey lamppost of grey East Germany.

But that almost honeymoon period came to an end and Jack started getting into trouble. There were instances where he was too heavy handed with a prisoner, or had deliberately walked across the parade ground or square, which was absolutely forbidden, regardless of rank. He started binge drinking again, getting a name for himself, and not a good one, in the corporals' mess. Marie's season of content had ended and straightaway her nerves were heightened. Her friends peeled away one by one, not wanting to be part of any of the drama that was unfolding, and she became very isolated again; and absolutely depressed. Most of the time she hated being pregnant.

Stacey, who had now become her closest friend and stuck by her, sat her down one day.

"You have to pull yourself together, Marie. You can't go on like this."

Marie was so unhappy and tears streamed down her face and dripped onto her fat belly.

"Jack was just like he was before we came here. From here on, it's going to be downhill, all the way to the bottom. And there's nothing I can do about it."

"Then I'll do something about it." And Stacey left speak to the families' office and told them they needed to do something about Jack and his alcohol. They just laughed and told her to tell Marie to fly home to the UK for support.

Even though she was severely depressed, Marie had her due date for the baby and her parents went over for the birth. In those days there were no scans that told you the sex so they had no clue if the baby was a boy or girl. Her parents, with her mother seeming brighter and her Dad less grumpy, had bought everything; pram, high chair, clothes and all the other things a new baby needed. Marie was eternally grateful about that because money was always tight with Jack pissing it up the wall.

Marie went into labour near the end of August. Things started very slowly and the British Military Hospital advised Jack not to bring her in until her contractions were five minutes apart. Eventually, after twelve hours of suffering through the agonies of early labour, with her parents in the living room watching TV and never once going into her room to ask if she needed anything, Marie ordered Jack to get off his arse and take her into hospital.

By then it was late at night, and she was put into her own room in the BMH. Although it was a lovely room and sported a beautiful view of Germany at the height of summer, Marie was in too much pain to look out of the window of her 12th floor room.

"Please, please, Nina," Marie implored the kind German midwife who was assisting her, "give me something for the pain. Anything, just make it go away." By now the contractions were coming hard and fast. Nina then proceeded to elaborate on how she had been working in Palestine for two years and was absolutely determined that Marie could do this naturally without pain relief.

"They don't haff any sort of pain relief in the fields of Paless-stein, ja!"

"Maybe they're just immune to pain," Marie tried. "They would find pain killers if they had to endure this..." and her voice trailed away as the next wave of pain engulfed her.

"Nein, nein. We vimmen all endure this, ja, and we don't die." Then she kept silent until the pain had subsided a little.

"Ve vill just help you along, ja," Nina said as she produced what looked like a long crochet needle. "Pliss spread your legs, ja. It will go quickly ven ve are done." Marie's waters hadn't broken yet, but with a quick poke of that needle it was a matter of seconds before she felt the gush of warm fluid. She vomited her thanks all over the gentle Nina.

"Gut, gut" was Nina's reply to the spray of vomit now all over her uniform. "Now it vill be quicker and more pain. Gut girl."

"Ugh," Marie groaned, as her contractions suddenly intensified. Nina had been right about the pain getting worse, so maybe she was also right about Marie not dying from it.

"Nein, Marie. You must not make noise. Keep noise inside off you and you vill have lots of... inside energy... for ven you vant to poosh."

Jack was hopeless and didn't even hold her hand as Marie now went silently through her labour. It was Nina who was the stalwart and ran a hot bath for Marie. While on her own having three minute contractions in that bath Marie, for the first time, silently whispered to the baby who she would soon meet. She said she was sorry. Sorry for ever making a baby to bring into this horrible world of worry and torture. With each contraction the bath water went very still. It was almost like the baby was acknowledging what she was trying to communicate.

By 3pm on the next day she was utterly exhausted. She had been in labour for about eighteen hours and pushing for two; something was clearly wrong. She was now in the delivery room with Jack and Nina and two military doctors. After a really painful internal examination the problem became clear. The baby's little fist was up against its cheek and every time Marie pushed, the baby would go back up the birth canal. This baby was also big, too big for a natural birth they thought.

One of the doctors suggested they would need to break the baby's shoulder to get it out and this threw Marie into a blind panic.

"Over my dead body!" she shouted even though she was exhausted and almost sleeping between the contractions. But Nina took her side and gave the doctor an evil look and said that if they broke the baby's shoulder it would cause all sorts of problems later in her life. So Marie braced herself and silently pushed for all her life was worth.

Eventually the head came but Nina screamed for her be silent. Marie was convinced that something was really wrong, and Nina explained that she needed to cut her to get the rest of her baby born because of the fist up against the cheek. Marie didn't even feel if the next contraction was coming, she grabbed Jack's arm and pushed, and pushed so hard her blood vessels burst in her eyes, which later made her look like a zombie.

Her baby girl, all 8lb 8oz of her, was born. Louise Amanda was perfect, all fingers and toes in place, everything normal apart from the fact she sobbed, very quietly, she was always quietly sobbing. Not screaming blue murder crying, but soft sobbing. It was really upsetting for Marie and worrying because she had no idea what was wrong.

Jack went home and brought Marie's parents in to meet their first grandchild. They cried, Marie cried, Jack cried and Nina just kept saying how proud she was of her "young English mom, ja."

The next day Jack arrived with miniature pink rose plant for her; ten minutes later Marie's parents bought a huge bouquet of flowers. Of course Jack was hugely pissed off with that, but the rose plant meant the world to Marie. It was the first and last flower he bought for her ... ever.

Marie's parents had to fly back to the UK two days after Louise was born. Her mother was devastated and tried to persuade her Dad to let her stay, but home they went. Marie didn't feel anything when they left, all she could think about was how was life going to change now that little baby was there.

Louise's arrival was not to be the only historic event that happened to Marie and Jack in Berlin. A couple of days before Louise arrived, Rudolph Hess, the Deputy Fuhrer to Adolph Hitler, died in nearby Spandau Prison, an apparent suicide. After his death the allies had certain duties to perform with the corpse. Each sector (British, French, American and Russian) had to identify and pronounce the death. His body was brought to the British Military Hospital in West Berlin for identification and death pronouncement and Jack, on a visit to Marie, shared a lift with it. This seemed very significant for Jack. He had actually seen the body bag with Rudolph Hess in it and saw this as a great piece of history. Marie felt he thought it more important than the birth of his daughter.

All military wives giving birth stayed in the BMH for seven days, but Marie was dying to get home. It was a Sunday when they released them and Jack came for them in the car. On the way home he told her not to be alarmed when they got to Spandau Prison, but to lock the back doors. Every British car in Germany had a distinctive number plate and could easily be identified as British. As they rounded the corner on their way to their quarter, they were stopped by a wall of demonstrating Neo Nazis at the gates of the prison.

They were mostly skinheads wielding banners and sticks. Jack slowly revved the car engine and a group of them started rocking the car. Marie was petrified in the back of the car, holding Louise in her arms. Then one of them noticed her and stopped his mates in their tracks. He shouted to them in German and they let the couple and their new baby through. They reached home and no one was there outside the block. Marie had wanted a fanfare, a welcome home, something, anything. Jack hadn't told anyone.

They introduced Louise to Bo, who never left her side after that first meeting. Marie loved her baby and her gorgeous boy, Bo. Bo loved Louise and she loved him. As he had seen Marie through dark times, she later was sure that he helped Louise, too.

BERLIN 'FAMILY' LIFE

I decided that it was time to spend some of the advance on our book and give us both a treat. I called Marie's lovely husband John and agreed that he, unbeknownst to her, could be OK on his own in the restaurant for a couple of days. I then booked us into the Chewton Glen Spa down in Hampshire. The story was getting worse and I wanted to give her some distractions as she relived her past with the awful Jack.

I arrived at her house, all packed and ready to go with my suitcase in my car. She opened the door and gave me a big hug as usual and then I stepped inside.

"You look dolled up hon" she said as I followed her into the kitchen.

"I know," I replied, dropping my car keys on the side, "we're going out."

"Really? Where to? I've got to go the restaurant later."

"No you haven't. We're going to Hampshire for a couple of days" I told her, unable to hide my grin.

"Hampshire? What's in bloody Hampshire?"

So I told her and she kind of freaked out.

"Ooh Tina! I love a Spa! And John knows?"

I nodded.

"You crafty bitch!" she said with a grin and then gave me a hug before she went to pack.

We were soon on our way and once I'd got onto the M3 I told her my tape machine was in my bag.

"May as well do some now," I said, "then we can relax once we're there."

"Sounds good to me," she replied, as reached behind my seat to get my handbag.

She stuck the recorder in the tray in the centre console and settled back in her seat.

"So... Berlin after the baby. Not good I guess?" I said as an opener.

Out of the corner of my eye I saw her nod her head briefly.

"Fucking understatement" she replied and then was silent. I concentrated on the drive and waited until she'd gathered her thoughts. By now she knew the kind of things I wanted to know.

"So there I was, only twenty one with a new baby daughter, in a foreign country and trying my best to cope with an alcoholic husband. Ten years older than me he was but behaved a lot of time like he was ten years younger. I'm dead sure that the stress that put me under was a huge factor in why I didn't bond with Louise when she arrived. I think I told you that before in Bali, right?"

I nodded and waited for to carry on.

"I was just really anxious all of the time and could never relax. While all my friends were enjoying the lifestyle forces families could have in Germany postings, going off buying stuff like electrical goods at cost, going to beer festivals or Christmas Markets I was stuck in the flat almost 24/7.

"You know Tina; I tried so hard with Louise, but I only ended up going through the motions with her that's for sure. You know, feeding her, bathing her, taking care of her needs as it were, but I was failing desperately in the nurturing side."

"Any idea why that was?" I asked and she waited before she answered.

"Looking back, I'd say my focus was always on him and what was he doing, loose cannon that he was. In some ways he was dead predictable, but in others he wasn't. Would he come home on time or would he stay in the mess? Would he come home pissed or would he get in trouble that day. Oh God Tina, it was all consuming and I guess because I had no support, no outlet for my frustration I was a bit like a robot- just coping with the mechanics of having a baby that I knew I had to 'care for'"

She waved her fingers in the air to highlight the inverted commas.

"He wasn't 100% bad; I have a photo somewhere of him asleep on the couch with Louise on his chest. When he was lucid and sober he was good with his daughter, but this wasn't very often..." She stopped and then laughed briefly. "You know there are no pictures anywhere that reflect me being a happy young Mum with my first baby. Can you believe that? I'm just bloody miserable on them all!"

"I guess that must have had an effect on Louise?"

"Oh God yes, it certainly did, but I'll have to come back to that later to give you the details. That's a big part of my story. Anyway, I only really left the flat for essentials and both me and Louise must have been really starved of just some plain, good old fresh air. But that was my life..."

She paused again and I could see her looking out of the side window as she reflected on her past once more. She turned back and I glanced at her as she gave me a sardonic grin.

"Here's an example for you. Christmas came and went with hardly a mention or change in routine. I did buy a few bits for Louise but she was far too young to have idea what was going on. All it brought, just as I expected, was even more drink and trouble. And then came New Year, which in a Scottish regiment was hell on earth. Jack disappeared 'First Footing' as they call it. To me it was just another excuse for him to be drinking himself into a state of oblivion. The rule is to leave the door open for anyone who wanted to first foot you. He had no friends other than his fellow drinkers who of course knew our door would be open so back he came with all of the idiots from the battalion who stayed for days just drinking.

"This was my life Tina" she said again. "It was the depths of a German winter, I had a baby who could have been the woman's up the street for all I cared and Jack was getting worse. I wonder now what the point of it all was, but then... not once did I contemplate leaving him. I just seemed to accept everything in my life as it was. I knew I was changing to become nothing like the Marie anyone else knew, but felt helpless to do anything about it..."

"Things got no better with Louise?" I asked and she shook her head.

"I had another friend, Lorraine who lived in the next block. She got a job in the NAAFI and asked me to start watching her little girl, Natalie. It gave me something to do. When Lorraine picked her up each day I was really jealous that Natalie, who was only two would get hold of her Mum's face with her chubby little hands and kiss her Mum right on the lips as if she hadn't see her for ages. She obviously loved her Mum and her Mum loved her. Even though Louise was only months old I somehow knew that she would never do that with me."

After that she went quiet and I asked her no more questions, just concentrated on the drive as the motorway got busier. Eventually she started talking again.

"Here's Jack for you again. One Saturday morning in February, Jack was sleeping off a heavy night on the couch and Louise was sitting on her potty chair watching him snoring when there was a knock on the door. Well that was highly unusual for that time on a Saturday, cos the corporals' mess didn't open until 12! Anyway I answered it and there stood the families' officer and I instantly panicked. When the families' officer visits where you live it can only mean one thing, someone's died, a member of either of your families, or at least been in a bad accident.

"My immediate thoughts were that it was my Dad since he was still a serving soldier himself; anything could have happened to him. Was he on a tour of Northern Ireland? I couldn't remember and I started to panic. Then the families' officer asked for Jack and I was even more confused as to why he was asking for Jack.

"Thing is Tina, he wasn't in touch with anyone from Airdrie really. His family was split up all over the place since their Mum's death all of those years ago. So now feeling dead embarrassed, I invited the officer into the flat and woke Jack up. I was stunned by what came next and how he reacted.

"So first of all he asked Jack to remain calm—the soft bugger of an officer must have known him!—and then he told us that one of Jack's brothers had called to let him know Jack's father had died."

"But hadn't Jack had anything to do with his father since he had walked out of the hospital room when his mother was dying?"

"That's right, but even so I didn't expect what happened next. Remember Jack had been lying down on the couch, but now he sat himself up and started laughing. In fact he was howling with laughter so the officer turned to me looking dead confused and I stared at Jack. He was laughing so hard it was of course infectious and Louise started giggling as well. But me—I was so bloody angry and all I kept thinking about was that he was such an absolute idiot and so embarrassing."

"Do you think now it was just his way of handling it?" I asked as moved out to overtake a big truck.

"Yeah I suppose so. Looking back now I guess it was some kind of release and I know people can deal with news of a death differently, but that families' officer was really taken aback. It seemed to me that he was more upset than Jack! He offered him a flight back to the UK for the funeral, but Jack told him to shove it. He even went as far as telling the officer he would piss on the grave when he next went home. Of course this guy didn't know the history and so he was dead was shocked by all this."

"I can guess what's coming next then" I suggested and she laughed.

"I'm bloody sure you can!" she replied and shook her head again at the memory. "I just stayed quiet because my mind, just like yours now, was way ahead of this. I knew it would be just another reason for Jack to go off on another major drinking session and of course I was right. After the officer had gone he made some excuse to go to camp and we didn't see him again for days."

"Arse" I said and she cracked up. I'd learnt that she appreciated my not getting all maudlin over her bad stories and that she liked it when I broke the tension. Eventually she carried on.

"So again I found myself drowning in anxiety, mechanically caring for my baby and living inside my own head if that makes sense. Time just morphed into one long stretch of shit, but if I thought this was bad it was heaven compared to our next posting!"

"Are we up to talking about that now or not yet?" I asked and she shook her head. "Oh there's more on Berlin to come yet," she said and then continued with the story.

"So what happened was that Jack came home one day in April full of the joys of spring for once. He sat me down and told me we were being posted away from the battalion to Penicuik on the outskirts of Edinburgh because he had been promoted to Sergeant! Not only a sergeant but the Provost Sergeant in charge of the army jail! I couldn't bloody believe it! To me he was a totally useless wanker and the Army fucking promotes him!

"Anyway, he told me we were off to the infantry training post at Glencorse Barracks in Penicuik. That's where the recruits to all of the Scottish regiments go to learn about being a soldier in the infantry and when I did go out before we left I found that this was a damn good posting in the eyes of any provost staff in an infantry battalion. But I also found out I was not alone in my views about the promotion; nobody could believe that he had got it! Everyone was absolutely gobsmacked and was asking how such an alcoholic could get a bigger and better job; most people expected him to get pushed back to being a bloody Private! Seemed it was beyond everyone apart from his bosses, but I know some of them were his drinking buddies! It was around that time he got his car repossessed because he'd rather used the money for his drinking."

"But how did you feel about going back to the UK?" I asked.

"Well, in my naivety I was quite optimistic when I thought about this new posting. I thought that surely if he was going to be away from the battalion with a very responsible job he would be better. I must have been off my bloody trolley!

"As the day grew ever closer to when we were to leave West Berlin I got increasingly worried and upset. Oh this was not because of Jack and his antics, but because of Bo, my beloved dog. Back then there was six months quarantine for any animals coming into the UK from abroad primarily because of Rabies. We knew we had to do this but I hung on and hung on and just wouldn't let him go at all; he was my life-line to sanity. In the end Jack found a lovely place ten miles from Penicuik and we were thinking we could visit him when we were there. Believe it or not, the thought of my dog in kennels all day long for six bloody months terrified me beyond anything I had ever been through..."

She must have caught my glance at this and knew I was thinking about the abortion early in her life and so on.

"I know it sounds daft Tina, but to me at that time it was true. I simply knew I would miss him terribly and who the hell would I talk too now about my shitty life?!"

"I actually felt like that about my hamster when I was seven" I said and she smacked me on the arm with a grin. "Soft bugger," she said before adding. "How long till we get there?"

"A while yet, but just take me to the end of Berlin and we'll stop there; it's time for a holiday!"

"Well sounds good to me! I've not had a pamper since Bali and that seems and age ago now. OK where was I? Oh yeah, Bo. Well one day I took Louise in her pram to be weighed and checked and when I got back Bo and Jack were gone, just gone for a walk I thought. There was no such thing as mobile phones then so after 3 hours of waiting I started to panic! When Jack finally came home he told me he'd booked Bo on a flight to Edinburgh to go to his kennels which was to be his home for 6 months. I was absolutely distraught that he has sneaked my baby boy away from me without giving me the chance to say goodbye and make sure he was OK.

"I knew he'd be stuck in a cage on the plane and taken to a kennel and wouldn't know he'd be without me for 6 months. I know he loved me as much as I loved him and with everything else about my life that day just broke my heart. It was torture not having him around and wondering if he was OK.

"I actually really hated Jack sometimes, but even more I hated myself for staying with him too. I worried about what sort of life the baby would have with us separated and so I stayed. Funny, but more importantly, I didn't want to be judged by Mum and Dad cos I knew I would be! How wrong is that? I couldn't stand the thought of them crowing over the situation so it was better to stay. To this day

I'm still like that. If me and John have a row, in all the 18 years I've known him, I have never once threatened to leave, he has many times—and he did actually leave once—cos I know I can be such a bugger to live with! Me though Tina, in the end I guess I'm just loyal..."

I stayed quiet as I let her gather her thoughts again whilst she stared out of her window again.

"I've thought about this before and I still reckon it's true. When you're living such a stressful life you cope on a certain level, but it has to affect you in ways you cannot deal with. Way before Louise was born, every day my anxiety levels were so bad that when I got pregnant I'm sure they affected the baby inside me. I don't quite know how and believe me I've analysed this and tried to research it. All I can say is that it's true that whatever the expectant mother experiences during pregnancy the baby will exhibit this when born. I'm 100% sure of that."

"I guess you can see that with hindsight, that if you had known you might have tried to be different?" I asked.

"Oh God yes, of course I would have!"

"What about the midwives. Did they not notice anything at your pre-natal classes?"

She shook her head before replying.

"In some ways, and certainly with them, I didn't want people to feel bad about me and so I had to put on a bit of a front of being OK so they probably didn't see any need. The other thing though is that even if I'd been happier when I was pregnant it probably wouldn't have mattered. Yeah Berlin was bad Tina, but little did I know that Penicuik would be even worse. I was so miserable there that it became the worst period in my life so far at that point, my darkest days when I would even contemplate suicide."

A SCOTTISH NIGHTMARE

Glencorse Barracks dates from 1803 and to Marie it seemed at times as if the place had never moved on. Nothing remains of the original house on the site from which the barracks grew, however, it is thought that the cellars of the Officers' Mess owe their existence to this 17th-century mansion. In more modern times the barracks went on to become the regional centre for infantry training for Scotland. Shortly before Marie and Jack arrived there a young corporal stationed there killed three Army colleagues in a payroll robbery south of Edinburgh. He was jailed for life and his three victims had all been stationed in Glencorse barracks as well.

This tale was told by Jack with what Marie thought as too much excitement, almost if he wished he'd been involved.

"I might be better off if he had been," she thought to herself as she gazed out of the bus window onto a grey and miserable day; it matched her mood entirely. "How free I'd be if the drunken bugger had got himself shot."

"So have you found out yet where we're living?" she asked him without turning away from her gaze at the passing Midlothian countryside. Louise was asleep on her knee and Marie was thankful the baby had mostly been quiet on the log journey.

"Oh ay love, I collared Sergeant McGregor in the lav when we stopped, we've got our own wee house with a garden."

He could have told her this two hours ago, but this latest news gave her a much needed boost as she imaged playing on a lawn with Louise in the summer sunshine; this brief respite from the depression she'd been feeling more and more did not last long. When they got there, their quarters were, as Marie told Jack, the fucking pits. It was a very old, small and dingy terraced house that smelt of damp and, at times, drains.

There was a small living room at the front and kitchen barely big enough for a small table at the back. Beyond that was a small bathroom which had clearly been converted to bring in the outside toilet. Upstairs were two bedrooms with threadbare carpets and curtains with no linings. As far as furniture and decorations went they were back to green, which was more than could be said for Marie's 'garden'. This was a brick-paved yard with a few dead plants sitting in either plastic or cracked pots.

So after arriving at their new posting, away from the battalion and not knowing anybody, Marie quickly realised this was not going to be an easy posting in the slightest; for Jack it was the opposite. He was now the Provost Sergeant in charge of the army jail in the barracks, which was the training depot for all Scottish Infantry regiments.

What soon transpired was that he was now in charge and this gave him a certain amount of leeway in what he did; Jack of course took complete advantage of the situation. Not only would he spend his time drinking with the provost Corporal, but all the inmates as well. There were two different guard rooms and he would hide out in either one, avoiding any higher ranks that might come by and would drink himself to oblivion on a daily basis.

The pressure this put on Marie was becoming intolerable and she avoided all contact with any neighbours. She knew this wasn't like her at all since, no matter how quiet she was, she always made friends. More and more it became the norm that all of her attention and efforts went into trying to prevent Jack from drinking and, she knows now, that nine month old Louise suffered from this without a doubt. Marie was just existing, going through the daily routines with no emotion inside her at all.

As much as she loved and sought to truly bond with Louise, it would take six months before Marie had a day where she felt truly felt happy; that was the day they went to collect Bo from quarantine. She was up around 4:00 am too excited to sleep. She fussed around making sure she got the best place for his bed, moving furniture to accommodate it and cleaned his food and water bowls until they shone. Eventually she dragged Jack out of bed around 7:00am, got Louise ready and they left soon after. Now they were on the journey, Marie reverted to her usual state and began to worry.

"You do think he'll remember me don't you?" she asked for about twentieth time that week.

"Oh fer fucks sake Marie, how the bloody hell would I know? You think I'm Barbara bloody Woodhouse or something?"

"Well you might at least try and guess and say something nice! I have to put up with your shit 99% of the time so at least today I was hoping for something different!"

Jack just muttered under his breath and Marie ignored him. She'd be seeing Bo soon and nothing was going to spoil that moment. They got to the kennels just as they opened and a young girl in a coat and wellington boots what were too big for her took them through a maze of kennels. A few dogs were quiet, but most barked and ran around; Marie dreaded seeing Bo just lying there suggesting he was unhappy. They rounded a corner and there he was; Marie immediately dropped to her knees and stuck her fingers through the wire. He gave a couple of barks at first and then seemed to drag something from his memory and immediately went berserk. He ran around a circle a few times and then, crying and weeing at the same time, he pressed his body to the wire and licked her fingers as if he'd not eaten for the whole six months. The emotions Marie had been suppressing for years came flooding out; Louise started to cry too not knowing what was going on and even Jack shed a tear!

Marie had her crutch back and would take him out on long walks every day with Louise in her pushchair. This made life a little more tolerable, but things with Jack continued to worsen. His drinking was completely out of control and he was spending every penny on his booze, so much so that money became really tight and he demanded that Marie find a job. She tried to find something within the barracks at first, but ended up working weekend shifts in a supermarket in Edinburgh. Leaving Louise with him was the hardest thing to do, but she was caught between a rock and a hard place.

Looking back now, she wonders how she ever got through her shifts; she was a complete bundle of nerves. Of course there were no mobiles then so she couldn't even send a text to make sure all was OK. She just had to keep watching the clock until her shift ended and she could get the bus home to see if the baby was OK and that he wasn't passed-out drunk. More often than not he was actually sober, but there was always the worry that he'd be the opposite when she got back. Maybe the temporary sobriety was down to the responsibility of looking after Louise, but whatever the reason, he certainly made up for it during the week at work.

Around the time that Louise turned one, Marie invited her sister Helen to come and stay with them for week. She thought it might be good for Louise to have someone else in the house that she might start to relate to; even this supposedly happy time added to Marie's woes. She came in from work around 10pm one night to find Jack snoring on the couch and Helen trying to tidy up the empty cans, fag ends and takeaway cartons that seemed to be all over the livingroom. What the hell had been going on here? Had he had a party? Had Louise been ok? What was Helens role in all of this? Just another episode of nervous angst, but this time involving her own sister!

She kept quiet about the incident, but for days she felt numb; it was yet another episode in her highly disturbing life with Jack.

This latest episode was the straw that very nearly broke the camel's back and in the following month, on two occasions, Marie very seriously contemplated suicide. She knew that everyone says it's a cry for help, but that was exactly what she needed, help! She had nobody she could turn to and nobody to even talk to her; she felt more distant from her own family than she ever had before, she even knew that she hadn't really bonded with Louise. Without any close family or friends she felt totally trapped and isolated.

On the second occasion when things got so bad she didn't want to carry on she even planned how she would take her life. She bought the tablets she would use and even planned what to wear. The day came... and went. At the last moment, sitting on the edge of her bed, she decided to do something positive instead. She called her Dad and asked him to come and get her and Louise. He thought she was coming for week's holiday with Louise, but no, she was leaving Jack!

It dawned on her that if she was so miserable that she had actually got to the point of suicide, she needed to leave him. He didn't have a clue what she was up to and she just waited for him to leave for work, knowing her Dad was on his way. She packed only a few bits and left; there were no mementos of her life with Jack, only bitter and twisted memories. She bundled Louise & Bo into her Dad's car with a false face on and off they went. She took a last look over her shoulder at the house she hated and wondered, if and when Jack came home that day, would he even realise they were not there?

She didn't feel anything on the three hour journey down south. Not only was she just feeling nothing and going through the motion of living, she also knew she was swapping one bad situation for another by going to her parent's house. In fact she was dreading having to interact with them at all and put on a brave face for a week. But she knew that if she didn't get a break from Jack she would very much succeed in taking her own life when she tried it again.

Quite surprisingly, Jack called her parents' house that night looking for her. When Marie took the call he was very upset and was begging her to come back; Marie just said no. Her parents were oblivious to this conversation in the living room playing with Louise. She wasn't upset or even angry, she just kept saying no. He stopped calling in the end after a couple of days, but Marie still changed her mind let her Dad take her back at the end of the week like he was expecting to. She felt like she was in limbo, not wanting to stay at her parents at all but not wanting to go back to Penicuik either. Life with her parents was no better and, in other ways worse. She had no means to escape whichever way she turned.

Throughout the journey back to Penicuik she was dreading going into the house in case there had been a party or something and even more evidence of how Jack really was. But she needn't have worried because he obviously hadn't been staying in the house; it was exactly the same as when she left. So immediately she now wondered where he had been. Her Dad stayed for a quick brew and left again, thankfully; she waited for Jack to come home for four days. He had just disappeared. She called the guard rooms, but his colleagues covered for him as usual.

When he eventually came home he was unrecognisable. He hadn't shaved or showered and he stank of alcohol. He was also in civilian clothing which told Marie he hadn't been on camp, but he couldn't tell her where he had been; he even seemed to have forgotten that she had left. At the sight of him in that state Marie was once again distraught. Years of anger welled up inside her and she was so disappointed in herself for coming back. Yet she was still anxious and nervous and all of those feelings were on the inside, screaming and crying out for help, but the outside person was functioning automatically. She was just a robot and went into auto pilot as usual. To everyone else she would have just seemed the same, very quiet and shy wife of *the* Black Jack as his mates called him.

It was a couple of days after this that she contemplated suicide again. Louise was sleeping and Marie was sitting on her bed with Bo. Just like before, she had what she needed to leave that torture, that so called life. This time she went a stage further and lined up the tablets along her bedside cabinet and got some water. She sat back against the headboard, with the first four tablets in her hand and then... something stopped her. Marie sometimes calls it divine intervention, but at that moment when she was really ready to leave and kill herself, her friend and long-time companion Bo raised his head and looked her right in the eyes.

For a long time they just looked straight at each other; he never wavered and neither did she. Marie doesn't believe in tales about animals knowing what you are doing, but swears that he saved her that day. Then there was what Louise did as well. After what seemed an eternity of her and Bo just staring at one another, Louise suddenly started crying. But this was crying like Marie had never heard her before. Until that time, just as she did the moment she was first born, Louise had only ever done her almost silent sobbing. But this was real guttural screaming and Marie leapt off the bed, tablets scattering all over the place and ran into the baby's room.

To this day Marie has no idea what had upset Louise so much. She was sitting up in her little bed and crying extremely loudly and reaching her chubby little arms out to her mother. Marie lifted her out and then she finally broke down. Mother and child collapsed in a heap on her bedroom floor, both sobbing like the world was about to end. Then of course Bo came in and was just................ there, like always.

Looking back, Marie realises it was a release for her, but is still not sure what the episode signified for Louise. But life went on regardless for the next five months, an endless hamster wheel of drinking, working and living only in her head. Then it happened. Jack got arrested by his own staff and jailed in his own military jail. She knew that would finally happen one day.

He had been caught drunk on duty and no one would cover up for him any longer. He was to be dishonourably discharged from the Army and very soon it seemed, which meant they had nowhere to live! Marie was numb. She wanted to get out of Penicuik for sure, but to be dishonourably discharged from the forces was a disaster. Would Jack get a job? Would Marie have to be the sole earner now?

Jack decided they would go to Bury where her Dad was serving his last couple of years in the Army. Since her brief visit her parents had bought a lovely 2 up 2 down house and her, Jack, Louise and, of course, Bo moved in. Marie actually thought it wouldn't be too bad, that Jack would behave there and she could work while her Mum watched

Louise. What transpired turned out to be a much greater nightmare than ever before.

BABIES, AFFAIRS AND A PRINCESS

"So am I in this book yet?" John asked as he brought over some coffee.

"Not bloody likely!" laughed Marie, "We're not putting you in it! I've told you already, it would ruin the sales!"

John grinned as he sat down at our table in their restaurant. Marie and I had just finished lunch and were just about to have another interview session.

"Well I thought you were going to use my photo on the cover to boost sales!" he said as he put out the cups and poured us some coffee.

I'd met John a couple of times before and I could see how happy they were, he was the perfect kind of guy for Marie and it was obvious to all who looked at them together that he absolutely adored her. A Scot and a few years older than her, he was quite laid back and an easy grin came to his craggy face. I knew they had their 'moments' of fiery disputes, but he was what Marie needed in that he never really put any pressure on her.

"Well I think that's a good idea!" I said and he winked at me.

"Oh don't you start Tina bloody Piper!" laughed Marie. "And you..." she added, turning to John, "can bugger off into the kitchen and leave us to talk about better men than you!"

"What? Drunken soldiers and your Dad? Well of course I can't compete there!"

"Exactly!" said Marie as she grinned at him.

We chatted a while longer as we finished the coffee and then John left us to it. The restaurant was almost empty now and we could record freely without lots of background noise. I took up the story from where we'd left it on the last session after we got back from the spa.

"So, you were back, in Bury, you, Jack, Louise and Bo, and living with your parents again?"

"Oh God yes! It was bloody awful. Nothing had changed with them—they still had this intense love/hate relationship that baffled me; it still does today really. So they had this lovely house, but I was afraid to even breath in it, let alone have Louise puke or something. My Mum was definitely going through the menopause or having some sort of hideous breakdown around this period, but we couldn't even sit on the couch without her shoving us forward and fluffing the cushions up!"

"So how were things with you and Jack now he was out of the army and away from all his mates?"

"Miserable mostly since I was having to watch his every move. I almost entirely left Louise to Mum and Dad, but really they took over with her before I even wanted them to. But that did make it easier to focus on Jack and try and control him.

However, he did get a job for a security firm and was more or less behaving, well at least while we were there."

"Did you need to work as well then?"

"Yeah I got a part time job in a card making factory, for Hallmark it was. It was fun and I met some nice girls there that I got on with. It was only a temporary contract so it didn't last very long, but it was nice having a 'life' of my own for a while and being able to breath. Well at least while I was out of the house I could!

"The thing is that as my anxieties lessened with Jack they increased with my bloody parents! Don't get me wrong Tina, I was really grateful they took us in, but I knew I couldn't live there long cos it would do my head in."

"Did you manage to get out quickly then or not?" I asked and she nodded her head over her glass of water.

"When a soldier and their family come into Civvy Street they get priority status with the council housing list. We knew we wouldn't have to wait long and soon got offered a shitty council house the other side of Rochdale. Much to Mum and Dad's—especially Mum's—disgust we took it, but I had to get out their place. What the council gave us really was awful though, a rundown 2 up 2 down terraced house in a bad street on a bad council estate.

"But Jack was getting quite good money from his job and he wasn't drinking it *all* away and so I was able to started making a home for us. I bought us some nice new curtains and decorated everywhere and inside it was like a show home when I had finished! But not as bad as my mother's, at least we could sit down and relax and leave the paper on the kitchen table!"

"So you were feeling happier?" She waited a few moments to consider her answer.

"Yeah a bit I guess, but inside me I was still void of any feelings, kind of still numb I suppose. Quite a bit depressed and anxious, but I knew I needed something to do, certainly after I'd got the house sorted; not working didn't help. Of course I had Louise to look after, but it wasn't enough for me and it gave me too much time to think and keep remembering how unhappy I was."

"I think you said in Bali that it was after Jack left the Army that Millie arrived. So did that happen when you were in the house in Oldham?"

"Yeah that and my world completely falling apart! It was around 4 months after moving into there that I found out I was pregnant again. I was really happy actually and so was Jack. I remember him saying that he might get a boy at last!"

She laughed ironically and shook her head.

"I thought the bastard was being too nice to me and then I discovered why. I found out that the shit was having an affair with a woman he worked with. Debbie her name was; another security guard. Up to then I had only had to deal with drink being the 3rd party in our... existence—I can't really call it a marriage—but this changed everything.

"The way I found out was horrible. He had just disappeared one day, gone out to work and then not come home. This was just like he used to do in the army and so I just presumed he'd gone on a bender and all of those old anxieties came rushing back, leaving me a wreck again and wondering where he was. On the third day Mum and Dad turned up at the door, which was very unusual. I thought something was wrong with Grandma Alice, but it turned out that someone who worked for the same company as Jack had tipped my Dad off that something was going on between Jack and a 'female colleague'. They were drinking in a pub in the middle of Oldham, still in their uniforms, when they were supposed to be at work.

"Dad was raging and he told Mum to watch Louise, but before we left he called and told my sister Helen to come as well as Mum was in a state too. As Dad drove us into the town my heart was in my mouth. I was newly pregnant and on my way, it seemed, to confront my husband and his fancy bit in a bloody pub! As we drove down the road where the pub was I spotted them in the beer garden together, laughing and joking and both drinking pints—I remember thinking, what a lady!

"Dad was just about to get the out of the car and I put my arm across his chest and told him I'd deal with it and he should stay in the car. I stormed over to them and screamed at Jack; I wanted to hurt him so badly in that moment. He was legless and just kind of looked at me at first. I ranted on about having to put up with his shit for all those years and then I started on her.

"It was almost a pleasure as I watched her jaw drop as she learnt, for the first time of course, that I was pregnant and had a 2 year old at home. Then I suggested that she was probably just a drinking buddy to him, but she came right out with it and, bold as brass, assured me they loved each other! Fucking cow! Well I told her to keep him and turned to go back to the car, but she grabbed my arm as if to start on me!

"Now that was when Jack really surprised us all. He told her in no uncertain terms to get her hands off me and we both walked back to the car, him more staggering than walking, where my Dad was waiting. By now he was out of the car and I had never seen him so angry. I poured Jack into the back of the car where he started rambling on in his pissed state. Dad just kept his cool and didn't speak all the way back to the house; that's when it all blew up.

"Once we were there, my sister Helen tried to sneak Louise into the car while Jack was in the loo, but he caught her. Ranting and raving, he grabbed Louise, who, no doubt frightened by all the noise, was really crying, and he told my Mum and Dad and Helen to leave and never come back. By this time I was a wreck in the living room and when they'd gone he simply plonked Louise on my knee. Then, without saying a word, he went to bed! I hated him more then than at any other time."

We stopped taping at that point for a while and, at my suggestion, Marie went to get herself a glass of wine from the restaurant bar. She'd surprised me with the way she was telling me this awful memory, there was little emotion which suggested that she'd really be able to move on from Jack. As she walked over she was simply shaking her head at the memories. She sat and sipped in silence for a few moments and then gave me a small smile and a nod to carry on. I turned the tape machine back on, but said nothing, waiting until she was ready. By now I rarely had to prompt her with questions, especially in the middle of something like that. After a drink of water she continued.

"So... I had a decision to make. Would I leave him now to go to Mum and Dad's or would I find the balls to lay down the law with him for the sake of keeping the family together? After a sleepless night, with no real decision made, I was in the kitchen having a cup of tea when he walked in. He quietly asked me to sit down at the table and then he spoke to me, from his heart, like he never had before.

"You know Tina, to this day I still believe that what he said that morning was the only occasion where he was ever 100% truthful and open with me. He explained he had indeed been having an affair with Debbie and that he'd slept with her. But he said that it wasn't about the sex, but that she was a drinker like him! That was what made her appealing to him, no nagging about drink, being with a kindred spirit—some fucking pun that is—instead of being with a miserable wife who hated him drinking. Believe it or not, I accepted that. Even though I could never understand his drinking, I did understand I was becoming awful to live with."

"What a piece of work!" I said, finding it hard to believe someone could think like that but also feeling really sorry for her at the time "So what did you say?"

"Actually not a lot! I was gobsmacked at first, but then just saw it as a way out. You know, I even thought that no one should be miserable, even Jack! So I offered him the get out. I told him he could go and be happy with her but that he would never see us again... and I meant it.

"Then he then dropped his next bombshell—he wanted to re-join his regiment and go back into the bloody Army! Without saying a word to me he'd been in touch with the recruiting office in Bolton and they had confirmed that he would actually be accepted back into the 1st Battalion Kings Own Scottish Borderers as a Corporal. I couldn't bloody well believe it! He said he felt lost in Civvy street and he'd been doing all of this over the last month and I didn't have a clue!"

"Oh my God! The rollercoaster continues! So what did you say?" I asked and she laughed out loud.

"You probably won't believe this Tina, but I decided I liked it best in the Army! I guess that it was because that's all I'd ever known and so I agreed with him that it would be the best for us! God Tina I was so naïve. I completely ignored any negatives of this move, but I was only 23. I had endured so much with this guy already and there I was excited about another move away from my 'family' back to the regiment. I must really have of thought of that as my actual family! I guess I was just totally mixed up.

"So after telling Mum and Dad, who went mad of course, we made the move up to Redford Barracks in Edinburgh to re-join the battalion. Jack was now in the intelligence platoon within the regiment—God there's a contradiction! The battalion was serving 6 months in Northern Ireland and he had to join them there, leaving me and Louise in our new married quarters. They gave us a decent 3 bed flat within a block of 8 and the people living there were mostly families of guys in the same battalion, but above me lived a girl called Lorraine whose hubby was a Para. He was based in Aldershot, but she was in that flat to be near her family.

"She had 2 girls and really became my best friend there. I was so much happier than being in bloody Oldham and then one day I bumped into Jenny! You remember her from Colchester? The one with the amazing wedding! It turned out that she lived in the block behind ours and she was now pregnant with her first.

"So actually it was great being back in the military environment and even better that Jack was away! It gave me time to breathe and sort myself out."

"He was away a lot then? The whole time they were in Northern Ireland?"

"Well he came home periodically, but his stint lasted longer than six months; the whole time I was pregnant really. The battalion came home, but Jack stayed as he was working in intelligence. So yeah, I was happy in those times as my belly grew and life was OK. I started Louise in nursery, but she absolutely hated it! She always cried and reverted to that silent sobbing when I left her, but I persevered. It was awful leaving her, but I knew it would do her good in the long run."

"So did Jack get home for the 2nd baby being born?"

"Yeah he did. He was away all that Christmas and I was due on the 20th of Jan and Jack got back for 4 days R&R on the 18th. Bless little Millie, she came in right on time! I went into labour in the early hours of the 20th and Millie was born at half five that morning. I say little, but she was an eight and a half pound bruiser; made my eyes water she did! She was nothing like Louise at all, with very dark hair and skin—very Italian looking! The minute I held her Tina I bonded with her and this was so completely different to when Louise was born."

"Do you understand why that is?" I asked.

"Of course I thought about that, long and hard, and what I decided, what I really do know now, is that it was because with Millie I had been on my own, with just Louise and Bo. That and finding new and old friends made me happy all the way through that pregnancy, with no anxieties or worries. It made such a difference and you know what Tina, she cried very loudly and a lot in those first hours and it was music to my ears."

"What about Jack after his comments about having a boy?"

"Actually he was really happy even though she wasn't a boy and only 5 hours after she was born we went home. I signed us out of the hospital because we were fine and I wanted to get back home to Louise, who was being looked after by Jenny. Louise was really smitten with her new sister and wanted to help me look after her all that first day, right until she went to bed—more bloody help than Jack was! Then, with our baby not even a day old, he, of course, had to go out to wet the baby's head.

"Jack was due to go back to Ireland on the 22nd and I honestly thought he would come home when the pub shut that night; but he didn't. It was 2 days before I saw him again when he turned up at the flat only 15 mins before he was due to be helicoptered back into N.I! But I didn't care, not one bit. I had my girls and Bo now and he could piss off forever for all I cared. Life went on for us without him and he hardly ever called me and never wrote a letter like a lot of the guys did."

We took a break there whilst Marie went to the kitchen to order us a cup of tea and when she came back she laughing so asked her what it was she'd remembered.

"I got the bastard back though a week after he left, but even that ended up back-firing on me. The Commanding Officer's wife turned up with a blue teddy and declared her congratulations to us on the birth of our new son! How bloody ridiculous! They couldn't even get the sex right so gave her the bear back and told her to fuck off! Word, of course, got out about this and Jack was summoned to see the RSM. To the army it was such a serious thing me telling her to fuck off that he actually got extra duties! Well it kept him off the drink for a month, but the problem was that also he wasn't allowed to go back to Ireland so we were stuck with him again."

A young guy from the kitchen came and brought our tea and once we'd both got a cup we got on with the story.

"When he got back he wasn't that bad to be honest. Of course he was out on the piss, for days on end if he could, but he did spend some time with the kids. Louise was starting to settle into nursery and Millie was just blossoming like her sister never did. When I thought back and compared them it broke my heart at times as I blamed myself a lot for the way Louise was. But overall I was a lot better and then, when Millie was only 9 weeks old, I heard that there was a vacancy for a new civilian telephone operator at Army HQ Scotland, just outside Edinburgh!

"You'll remember how much I had loved that job in Warminster when I was 16 and God knew we needed the money so I applied for it and got it! Jenny offered to have the girls for me and all of a sudden I had a life! It was brilliant. I had money, a social life, my girls and Bo and a husband as little as possible! It was a really happy time for me."

"So that must take you towards when the first Gulf War was declared?"

"Yeah right and the biggest memory there is another bloody Jack episode! My Dad was OK and we knew he definitely wouldn't be going, but there was lots of talk about whether Jack's battalion would go or not. August came and went, so did September and by now I was on shifts and was sometimes doing nights. With what might happen Jack seemed focused and looked after the girls and the drinking wasn't as bad. But then we got word the whole battalion would be going to Iraq or Kuwait."

Marie finished her tea and then started laughing.

"I guess it sounds awful, but while the other wives in my circle were frantic with worry I actually relished the thought of Jack going off to fight in a war! With him a long way away I could continue to live a happy life, in fact no matter where he was in the world, at war or not, I had my friends, money and my little family unit and that's all I wanted.

"Anyway the next of Jack's finest hours surrounded the night before he left when he invited his sister and husband to come to have 'a wee swallie' to send him off... what a fucking bastard! I took the girls and the dog into the bedroom whilst they all got pissed. Can you imagine that? The night before he goes off to war he wants to spend it with his drunken family instead of with his wife and children?"

I simply shook my head and let her continue.

"God I felt so humiliated and worthless. Then to cap it all he gets so pissed he starts a fight with a neighbour and when some others complained about the noise he got arrested by the military police! They only kept him in the jail for 3 hours cos of him going to war the next day. That's just another day in the life I had to endure with him.

"So off he went and peace and quiet, even with 2 kids and a dog and working full time, returned and I felt much happier. I hadn't learned to drive yet, but Jack had left his car with one of the lads in the rear party, like a stand-by, and he'd been instructed to take me to work or shopping whenever I needed him; his name was Kenny and he became part of my routine of work, kids, dog, work, kids, dog and it was all I wanted and needed... well it was until one night on the way home from work when he told me how he felt, about me!

"Well of course he just knocked me sideways! I was so shocked because for so long all of my energy and focus, as far as men were concerned, was on Jack. Having had two kids it never occurred to me that I would be attractive to other men. He was married too, with a son, but all of a sudden I found myself embroiled in a very steamy affair! The first I'd ever had.

"He would come to my flat whenever he could as long as the girls were asleep. It was fantastic at the time and I had no care for any consequences if Jack, or even Kenny's wife found out. It was weird Tina, as though I became this rebel, this person my parents certainly would not have recognised. I started going out with Lorraine every night from Thursday to Sunday, leaving the girls with Pam another neighbour. I finished it with Kenny because all of a sudden there were other men, lots of them! I still say I had the time of my life when Jack was in the Gulf war!

"The reports were coming back all the time about which of our poor guys got killed or wounded, but because I worked on the telephone exchange we got the news first, so I was in the know about which unit had lost one of their own. In the end he was away for 9 months and I took full advantage. I slept with loads of guys and I make no apology for this either, I had great fun and was getting loads of attention! It also felt like I was getting revenge for all the shit Jack had put me through. Don't get me wrong, I never went out until the girls were settled and asleep and every minute I was with them was real quality time. They wanted for nothing emotionally from me during this period because I had a perfect balance of happiness, confidence and self-esteem; it was just heaven!"

She paused for a moment, looked at me and then grinned.

"You don't think I..." she began and I put a hand on her arm.

"I think nothing of the sort," I replied. "You had to push back on him at some time and somehow, and how you did that cannot be judged and anyway, the best way to do it was to have some fun!"

"Thanks Tina!" she said with a wink and I gave her a smile and a nod of encouragement.

"OK where was I... oh yeah, another *very* happy time and this one totally different. It was while the battalion was away that I met the totally wonderful Princess Diana! I'd loved her since she first appeared on the scene, and sat glued to the TV when she got married. Then Will and Harry came along and I watched her blossom into a wonderful mother. Meeting her was a dream come true. It really was."

"So how did that come about? Did she visit Jack's regiment?"

"Yeah that's right; she came to visit the wives when our hubbies were away. To make it fair, every wife's name was put into a hat and the commanding officer picked one wife from each rank from the privates up to the officers. They told us all about two weeks before she was due to come and I so, so wanted to get the chance just to be in the same room as her, if only for little while. Lots of the other wives were quite laid back about it, but I was getting myself totally wound up. Of course I was convinced that I'd never get the chance, so when I was picked for Jack's rank I really couldn't believe it! I was running round the house like an idiot and the kids must have thought I'd gone crazy!

"Anyway, I couldn't sleep the night before I was so excited and on the day I dressed the girls in the same outfits—beautiful red barrack coats with matching little berets. They looked fabulous! We were bussed from our married quarters to the officers' mess ballroom and the 10 or so wives and their children had to line up in order of their hubby's rank. There was lots of nervous chatter as we waited for her to come in and the CO and his wife—her of the blue teddy bear who never looked at me—were there along with a lot of security and the military press people.

"Louise was hugging my leg and I was holding a chubby Millie, then there she was! I tell you Tina, the room fell silent and we all just gasped. She was so absolutely beautiful and I was just mesmerised. Being how she was, she bent down to speak to each child before acknowledging the mother and it just struck me as being so natural. It's what any mother would do, never mind a royal! Then it was our turn and all of our practice for the curtsy, well mine and Louise's, paid off and we managed it beautifully!

"Louise presented her with a small posy of flowers we'd had made and she thanked Louise profusely which sent her into a spiral of shyness and she clung even harder to my leg, burying her face! The princess gave the posy to her lady in waiting then turned her attention to Millie. She was stroking my baby's cheek and cooing at her before she spoke to me. She first asked my first name and told me I had 2 adorable daughters. She then leaned in very close to me, taking my hand and said, "I really would love a little girl." She was beaming as she said it and I can only describe her as an angel. She was serene and beautiful, gentle and shy and I still count that as one of the most meaningful moments of my life.

"I tried for years to get copies of any of the pics taken that day by the military photographer, but never was able to. They must be archived somewhere but, I guess I'll never see them. I just consider myself a very lucky lady to have met her before her death. All they said about her was true Tina; she was indeed the people's princess."

THE FINAL STRAW… OR NOT

"You want another glass?" she asked me and I shook my head. "Better not. I'm driving, but you go ahead."

"Too bloody right I will!" she replied with a grin. "I need to get pissed when I'm talking about that useless shit!" She went to refill her wine glass at the restaurant bar and then we carried on.

"So how long was he away for?" I asked.

"Nine blissful months!" she replied, laughing. "Nine months and I never heard a sodding word from him, not even on a military line, but I didn't really want to talk to him anyway. Life just carried on, me working, looking after the girls and going out when I could. It was great and I was loving life during this period.

"Yeah but all too soon—well at the least for me—the men were coming home and all the families were transported to the camp in big buses to wait for them. I really didn't know what to expect cos we hadn't seen or heard from Jack in such a long time. So the buses started turning up and there were all of these loving husbands so happy to be reunited with their wives and kids. I was feeling apprehensive cos Jack had never been the tactile demonstrative type so I wondered what he would do.

"Anyway, he was one of the last off the very end bus—I almost started to think I'd got lucky and he wasn't there!—but as he stepped down I knew it was him straight away. He was sun tanned and looking thinner than I had remembered him and so I waved and said to Louise to run to Daddy; she clung to my leg. He spoke to Millie first, and then Louise before he gave me a kiss on the cheek; that was it. For all the other wives and kids it was huge hugs and getting spun around. Again, I was left wanting."

"Did that upset you?"

"Not really. It was not that I wanted a hug and stuff from him as such, but more that I yearned to be with someone who wanted to hug me, someone who cared about me... bastard!

"Anyway, the wives were shuttled back to the quarters to wait for them coming home from their various de-briefing meetings and he actually turned up at tea time which surprised the hell out of me. I was expecting him not to come home, but then I learnt the reason why he had when he just dumped all his smelly kit home in the middle of the living room floor... what a twat!

"I'm sure all the other wives would agree, but when you've been living without the men for so long you have everything spic and span and neat and tidy then they come home and completely invade your space. That's bad enough, but when you have no relationship to speak of it's even worse! I just felt... oh I don't know... maybe invaded is the best word.

"Then it turns out that the guys had one week's leave—only one week!—I couldn't believe it. They'd been away fighting in a war, seeing their mates die and get horribly injured, and when they come back they've got just one week to get it out of their system. Well I learned a lot in that week—Jack was most certainly *not* the person who had gone away; not at all. He was subdued, quiet, unapproachable and sullen and most of all he was angry... very angry. He was even drinking in the house now which he'd hardly ever done before and I didn't want the girls to see what he was like so I called mum and dad. I lied and told them me and Jack wanted some time together and asked if they could take the girls for a while, which they did.

"I kept going to work not knowing what I would find when I got home, but more often than not he would just be sat in front of the TV with cans of beer and a bottle of Bell's Whiskey. Then one evening I found him sobbing in the corner of Louise's bedroom—that was very scary and I really didn't know what to do; he wouldn't let me near him at all. In the end I called the families' officer who simply said that they had seen a lot in the war that would have affected them and just to be patient. Of course now we know more about Post Traumatic Stress Disorder, but back then we didn't know what was happening.

"So back came the stress and anxiety, but now it was actually born from worry and not hate; it was completely alien to me to be worried about him and not angry at him. We all struggled on, some of the other wives telling me of their husband's problems as photos emerged of Iraqi soldiers burnt in tanks, of bodies in the sand. Us wives could never really comprehend what they went through over there.

"Jack went back to work and back to a drinking routine, but things remained different. He was now extremely aggressive with the other guys and even the higher ranks and was jailed a few times for starting fights and punching guys for no reason. It was back to humiliation for me and he started disappearing again. I remember being at work on the exchange one day, my girls with a friend, when he called me after being missing for two days. He told me he had been 'lost' for those two days and didn't know where he was or how to get back! I had to leave work and try and find him, but when I got home he was already there. Crying in a corner again and I just didn't know what to do.

"The days and weeks went on after that in a nightmare of drink and violence. Never actually against me, but the house got trashed many times over this period.
He even started getting into scraps with best friends and this was terrible as their wives started to avoid me too. Not that I had many friends really, but for the ones I did have for a bit of support to turn their backs on me was just awful."

"So there was no respite at all then when you were at home?" She shook her head sadly and too a large gulp of wine.

"I was fully aware of how much Jack had added aggression to his drinking and so were his higher ranking colleagues. He was gaining a real reputation as both a liability and hard man. Some of the guys tried it on with him on a daily basis and he would generally knock them out! But, perhaps even more than the drinking, I hated this in him because I hate violence of any kind after being witness to dad in his drunken days in Germany, attacking mum for no reason.

"But Jack never ever laid a finger on me or the girls, I have to give him that, but he really was unrecognisable as the same person to anyone. He lost all of his mates and no one wanted to be around him. Then we got told of the battalion being moved to Weeton Barracks in Blackpool and I hoped a change of scene might do him good, but it didn't... worked out better for me though!"

"Oh yes?" I asked and she grinned over her wine glass. "In a minute!"

I smiled and decided that half a glass of wine would be OK when she got up to fill hers again. I wasn't sure if she was getting a bit pissed, but I didn't think so; she'd drunk me under the table on a few occasions after that first night in Bali. I started the tape again.

"They gave us our married quarters right out on the boundary fence of the camp—out of the way I guess—in a row of 8 houses. Lots happened in Weeton including some strange and sad accidents. One of our young lads got drunk and ended up comatose in some bushes and died of hypothermia and then one of the staff sergeants wives died after running over the lawn mower cord when she was cutting the grass in her garden. That was a real shock to us all cos Claire was a friend to everyone and was sadly missed. Her hubby Charlie is still a friend on Facebook; he's a security advisor in the Gulf now, but he has never re married. The guys were still going to Northern Ireland for 6 month tours and it was whilst Jack was away that I started a long affair with Mike!

"He was from the same town in Scotland as Jack and had a wife and two kids, but the chemistry between us was palpable. Every Mess do we would furtively catch a few minutes at the back of the building for a fumble and a snog. God Tina we were like a couple of bloody teenagers! He was lovely and looking back I think he felt sorry for me being in the situation I was with Jack.

"I remember one night we had arranged for me to pick him up—I'd passed my driving test the year before- so we could go to a hotel in Blackpool for a proper night of passion. I got someone to look after the girls, said I was going to see my parents and went to pick him up as arranged. I was all dolled up with suspenders and stockings and then he declares he has to get home to his family!

"I was devastated because in my naivety I thought this was going somewhere. I guess I had hung on to a dream that life could be good beyond Jack, but to Mike I was just a shag. I'm not sure if this was right or wrong Tina, but this was to become a pattern in my life. I was using my looks and sexuality to get attention, but I was attracting the wrong type of attention. I guess my view was that any attention was good..."

I said nothing because I'd told her that, no matter what she told me I was not there to judge her. This was her story and it was simply my job to tell it. After a few moments she simply shook her head and pushed her half full wine glass out of the way.

"Louise started school on this posting and hated it of course, but Millie loved nursery being the laid back kid she was. I got a part time job in a hypermarket in Kirkham selling costume jewellery and other kinds of tat. I liked that job and it was good money, but someone had their eye on me for something else. On the camp there was what we called a sweetie van that drove around every night. It was a little mobile shop, crammed with everything from dog food to penny sweets, fags and booze.

Well the owner, Pauline, was nearing pensionable age and was fed up with coming out at night in all weathers so she asked me if I wanted to take it on. I jumped at the chance because it was just what I needed. I was in control of something in my life and earning money again that I was determined wouldn't be pissed away. We asked for one of the camp garages that were behind our house and every night the van was locked up there.

"Jack watched the girls and for a while and he actually seemed responsible and it was working out fine, but of course it didn't last and he soon got fed up. One night I was locking up the van when my neighbour came out with the dog and the two girls in tow. I knew straight away he was on the piss somewhere so I put the girls to bed and waited. He came home after three days, a right bloody mess... literally. He had been in a real scrap somewhere and he was cut and bruised and bloodied, reeking of whisky and totally legless. He fell up the stairs as if going to the loo, but ended up in the girls' bedroom.

"What happened next still makes me sick today Tina—the bastard actually pissed on Louise in her bed thinking he was in the toilet. I can't describe the hot anger that rushed through me in that moment—I wanted to kill him. I was trying to manoeuvre him out of the room and trying to console Louise who was awake and crying by now, but then he was sick on the end of her bed too! At that moment I hated him so much more than I ever had before.

"I grabbed Louise and ran to our bedroom and placed her on our bed. As I went out of the room to see what he was doing he was staggering at the top of the stairs and... well I'm not proud of this Tina,

but I put my leg out in front of him and he fell head first down the stairs and landed at the bottom in a heap.
There was total silence and I thought I had killed him and in that split second.............I actually nearly shit myself!"

She wiped a tear and shook her head again; I said nothing, but of course I was desperate to find out what had happened next. Then she laughed.

"No such bloody luck! The bastard started moaning and moving around a bit so I just left him there. I got Millie and locked myself and the girls the dog in our room for the night. The next day when I got up he was in the kitchen, but he didn't speak to us at all and we never said a word to him. He mooched about the house as if he had the weight of the world on his shoulders and later that day he was arrested by the military police for punching the Regimental Quarter Master. I didn't know how much more could I take.

"To this day Louise has never forgotten that incident and as an adult now she doesn't speak to her dad, stating that disgusting episode as one of the reasons. Two hours after the arrest my dad called me to say my beautiful grandma—mum's mum—had died. My priorities changed in that moment and I couldn't give a shit about Jack then, so I left for mum and dad's after I called the families' officer to ask him to let Jack know what had happened and that I was with my family. Of course I couldn't grieve with my family for my grandma, Jack saw to that.

"On the day before the funeral of grandma I got a call from one of my neighbours and she told me that Jack had broken into the garage where the sweetie van was stored and had nicked all of the fags and booze and was selling it around the camp! My dad was raging and wanted to kill him, but I was determined to get there first. I left the girls with them and drove back to camp, but he was nowhere in sight. I went back to the house and there on the kitchen worktop was a letter—a letter from that cow Debbie who he'd had the affair with those years ago.

"Well the gist of it told me that they had been in touch since he had re-joined the battalion and the letter was full of the words love and missing each other. Now I really saw red and started knocking on doors until I eventually found him at his newest drinking pal's house. There was a real houseful, all of them pissed as farts and there were loads of young girls there too. I forced my way into the living room and punched him straight in the face, so hard that he reeled back and fell onto the couch.

"Years and years of anger, upset and frustration came out that day, but I was very calm, all the time looking him square in the eye when I told him I was going to kill him. He must have known I meant it because he seemed to sober up right away and hauled me out of that house as quick as he could.

"Not only did I have the embarrassment of trying to make excuses to my grieving family, but I had to pay Pauline for the damage and missing stock from the van. Yet again my dad told me to leave Jack and still I said no and just buried my head in the sand and carried on. Then one day, not long after, I was shopping in the NAAFI on camp when one of the commanding officer's clerks stopped me, asking if I had heard of the options for redundancy that were currently sweeping across the Army. Of course we had all heard about this, but had no idea if would reach our battalion; that's when he hinted very strongly that Jack was going to be given compulsory redundancy because they'd had enough of him.

"So at last some good news Tina. I had no idea how much he would get, but knew it would be a lot. Eventually he was offered £64,000 and within 6 weeks we were again heading for Civvy Street to live with mum and dad again.

CIVVY STREET

Marie found the prospect of moving on from Army life exciting, but even though she'd had as much as she could stand from its trials and tribulations, it was still a bit frightening to make that leap. She was filled with worry about what would come next; where would they live, would they find good work, would the girls be happy?

Their first taste of civilian life in so many years was in Marie's parents' home. It was a tiny two up two down and the experience was certainly not pleasant for anyone. All six were cramped into two bedrooms and Marie was certain her mum was going through another breakdown. She was extremely hard to deal with and was constantly embittered about her over-neat home being "wrecked" by an active young family. Her mum could barely handle an askew sofa cushion let alone kids' toys and dropped food.

But Marie was pleased to be close to her Grandma Alice, whom she clearly adored. She would pack her girls up and they would adventure over to her home; it was a welcome respite from her mum's moaning about so-called messes. Grandma Alice was always warm and welcoming and she understood Marie on a level she just couldn't get from anyone else. Millie and Louise were shy at first, but soon warmed to Grandma Alice's cosy home. At Marie's approach the front door would be thrown open and the trio greeted with an enthusiastic, "Come in, come in."

"Your mum'll not be pleased you abandon her so often in favour of comin' 'ere!" Grandma Alice said one morning, giving a knowing smile.

Marie could only give a guttural "Ugh," as she happily just dumped her bag on a chair and greeted Grandma Alice with a hug and a kiss on the cheek. Marie noted the soft wrinkled flesh and tried to banish thoughts of Grandma Alice getting on in life. Those worries were for another time as Marie and her grandma gossiped about goings on and Marie chased the girls into the back garden so they wouldn't break anything in the house.

Back at the tiny house Jack was behaving himself and Marie knew it was because he was living under her dad's roof; Jack had even got himself a good job working as a driver. The search for a place of their own began and they arranged for a mortgage advisor to visit at Marie's mum and dad's. The money they had nestled in the bank provided a big cushion and, for once, allowed them to be in charge of their own fate. A mortgage was quickly arranged and Jack and Marie were soon settled on moving into a lovely house two streets away from her parents. It was at this point she began to feel distinctly uneasy.

Being saddled with a mortgage with Jack wasn't that bad, it was the close proximity to her parents that had Marie unnerved; she knew it was a disaster waiting to happen. She and Jack were in the cramped space of the room they shared with their daughters, the girls' sleeping peacefully on the floor, when she broached the subject.

"This house..." she began and her tone immediately sent off alarms off in Jack and his head jumped off the pillow.

"Out wi' it!" Jack ordered.

"Do you think we ought to live so close to my mum and dad?"

Jack watched her as she spoke and it seemed that he was expecting something else, so she added, "and you know dad has never liked you... well that is... me bein' with you."

"We just got everything settled. What do you expect to do now if we're not moving into that wee house?" Jack asked, but he didn't seem that pissed off.

"Can you imagine coming home from work and mum and dad are at the table eating with us and me mum's..."

Marie never got to finish the sentence as Jack now readily agreed with her. She wondered why dealing with problems with Jack couldn't always be as easy as that.

So they decided to go to the council and, for once, were very lucky when they were allocated a brand new association house; Marie was almost equally happy that the place was fifteen miles from her parents. For all of her mum's constant fussing and moaning about her house being out of sorts she was completely awful when moving day arrived. She was especially unhappy with Jack about him getting his way.

"Well *you* must be happy," she said to Jack as he passed her with armfuls of their belongings.

Little did she realize that it was Marie getting *her* way, since being two streets away would have been awful. Marie had many regrets in her life, but this was not one of them. When she looks at why this was so out of the question for her she realises that it was because she didn't want to ever have to explain any drama that was inevitable in her life.

They settled into their cosy home and, for a while, life looked up. Jack was working, the girls were in school and Marie was dead happy when she got a good job on the telephone exchange at a local haulage company close to their home. They even managed a family holiday to Corfu, staying in a tiny bed and breakfast hidden between huge resorts, but Marie didn't even mind they couldn't afford the posh places.

In the mornings, the proprietor's wife fussed over them and she made sure they never left without full stomachs before they headed for the beach. The girls loved to play in the sand and chase in and out of the sea, and Marie's heart was especially delighted to see Jack build sandcastles with Louise while she lay in the sun after slathering sun screen on Millie. The sound of Jack's voice actually speaking in loving tones towards his daughter and the little peals of laughter that issued afterwards were the loveliest of sounds to Marie. Depeche Mode had nothing on that.

"Where shall we go next? Paris?" Marie asked jokingly as their trip came to a close. Jack laughed as Marie dumped wet and sandy cozzies into a plastic bag.

"Oui, oui mon cherie." Jack joked in a very bad French accent. After a pause he added, "Le singe est la-bas." Marie waited for translation—the monkey is over there—and then laughed. "It's the only thing I can remember," Jack said with a grin.

Back home again, the company where Marie worked were recruiting some more drivers and Jack got a job there, overall he was behaving well enough if not on his best behaviour. Marie made new friends and once again began enjoying a social life. Six months went by and Marie finally felt free to lower her guard, but quickly learned that was a mistake because that's when Jack struck again.

Weeks went by but he'd just disappeared, leaving her to wonder what the hell he was up to. When he finally returned home he reeked, saturated with a thick scent of drink and filth; it was even as if he'd been 'dug in' again as he had in the Army in Ireland. Marie would later learn that Jack was spying on his ex-wife and he's been watching her from a hole in a hill overlooking her house in Glasgow. To some it might have sounded crazy, but to Marie it was the PTSD playing havoc again.

It was a couple of months after that when, early one morning, Marie was dragged from a deep sleep by an insistent pounding. Bleary eyed, she looked out the window and couldn't believe what she saw: three vans and a car full of police. She wondered straight away if this was yet another thing to do with Jack, but he was at work on a run in the lorry and she was alone with the girls. Could the police presence at her home be a mistake? What could he have done now?

She threw on her dressing gown and hurried down the stairs as the banging on the door persisted; the minute she opened it a sheet of paper was thrust into her face by a burly man with a crumpled blue suit. In his other hand he held up his ID.

"I'm Detective Sergeant Burns and I have a search warrant for these premises."

"But why?" she stammered as she felt the girls come up behind her and each cling on to a leg.

"We've had your husband under observation and we have good cause to believe that he and another driver have been stealing meat they were supposed to be delivering and reselling it."

Marie's heart dropped and her mouth went instantly dry; she could very well imagine that what they said was true. She and the girls were ordered into the living room and helpless, confused and scared she had to wait as their home was torn apart by the search.

Marie was devastated by the news, thinking about her co-workers and recalled the times she'd enjoyed being with them while working at the haulage company. She loved her job and now she was left totally humiliated by her husband's selfish decisions.

Eventually the police left but a short while later she got a call that Jack had been arrested and was being held at the station. Then the gruff sergeant came back and Marie was questioned for what seemed like ages. He did not believe her at all that she didn't have the slightest idea of her husband's criminal activities and all the family's meat was taken from her freezer as 'evidence.' She had bought it only that week at Asda. Once again she felt violated by Jack's continued self-destructive activities and now she'd been further violated by the police who were unwilling to believe her side of things.

The police had been gone for several hours before Marie finally called her dad, but he came without hesitation to pick up his granddaughters, leaving Marie with some time and space to think; the next morning she called her boss and resigned. There was no way she could face her colleagues again after what Jack had done; she would never be able to survive the humiliation. Her manager was reluctant to let go such a good worker and Marie was encouraged to stay despite the troubles with Jack, but she couldn't face them.

Jack finally came home later that day with a story that Marie knew was a complete pack of lies. As well as taking the meat he had robbed Marie as any semblance of an ordinary life evaporated and all the happiness of the previous months was gone.

"You're such a selfish bastard," she'd said after he'd finished his diatribe. "And you've no fuckin' back bone either. Can't even tell me the truth!"

"Oh don't start on me woman, I've had it from the polis all fuckin' night and all I want now is a wee drink." It was at that point that Marie dumped her still warm coffee over his head and marched out of the kitchen.

For tea that night she made Jack a wonderful pie......................using Bo's dog meat as the filling. Weirdly Jack said it was the best pie she had made, in his drunken stupor!

Another few months went by where things between the two were still really strained. Jack had not worked since then and nor had she and that, combined with his continually excessive drinking, meant that all their money was just about gone;' but things were about to look up.

Marie was on her way back from the school run when she bumped into a neighbour, a good friend of theirs called Albert. He noticed that Marie was upset, another row with Jack who had just got home paralytic and asked if she was OK; at the question Marie just burst into tears. Albert gave her his snowy white handkerchief and once they'd sat down on a bench at a nearby bus stop she recounted her burdens with Jack. Albert just listened and never passed any comments or judgements, but Marie felt a lot better in having someone to talk to.

Eventually they went their separate ways, but Marie was surprised to find him knocking on their door at six o'clock that night. Luckily Jack was sober and in a better mood and the three settled down at the kitchen table with a pot of tea. Albert asked about the girls and spoke of his own family, his kids now grown and made it very clear to Jack that it was time for him to really accept his responsibilities. Jack looked pissed off at first at getting another lecture, but Albert seemed to handle him really well. It was then that Albert dropped his bombshell.

"So you'll need to get another job then Jack?"

"Aye, I know. I have been lookin..." he lied, but Marie managed to bite her tongue; she wanted to see where Albert was going with this.

"Well I think I might be able to help you out."

"Oh aye?"

"Yeah well, you know I have me own window cleanin' business and it's goin' well so I was thinkin' of expandin'. I've got a good reputation and another bloke who's been busy in our parts has just had to pack it all since he's got cancer poor bugger. Any road, I wondered, Jack if you wanted to come into business with me?"

"Well... how do ya mean?" asked Jack, looking dumbfounded.

"As a partner like. You'll be self-employed and work your own areas, but we'll agree to put so much into the business. Pay for us vans and ladders and advertising and the like and keep some back for the future, but then the rest goes in your pocket."

And that was it. Within a couple of days Jack and Albert were working together and Jack seemed to really enjoy it. He cut back on his drinking, got up early most mornings and grew the business with some nursing home contracts and other big properties. The money was good and Marie was even more relieved when Jack actually went to the doctor for help with his drinking and he was given Antabuse medication.

The PTSD remained a constant visitor causing bouts of emotional upheaval, but that, without him drinking, was somewhat more tolerable and, for the most part, things seemed to settle down. The drugs took a bit of time before they kicked in, but soon any alcohol consumption while on the pills made him violently ill and he was unable to even use aftershave or mouthwash. Jack being Jack, he wanted to test the efficiency of the Antabuse and he was sick for weeks after that. He lost weight, complained of pain and was lethargic and a part of Marie thought he was exaggerating his symptoms. Then they discovered that he also had an ulcer so to some degree his condition had been because of that.

Despite his working again, all of the problems with Jack were bothering Marie from a further aspect: the girls were growing like weeds before her eyes, developing so quickly, but she was missing so much of it. Her mind was always veering into Jack's path and her worries for what havoc he would bring on them next was her own ulcer to deal with.

But some sense of normality returned when Marie got a job at the local college, working on their switchboard, and again she felt the vivacious rush of what it could be to thrive. Marie enjoyed new friendships and a steady income and the work also provided a reprieve from the unsettling and unstable atmosphere at home. It was a palpable thrum that suggested that any minute things could again take another turn for the worse, but at work Marie had the chance to be productive and useful, and let her mind rest on other duties.

However, as seemed usual in her life, there were more problems and complications as Jack's PTSD began to worsen. One minute he would be quiet and sullen and the next there'd be tirades and dreadfully angry outbursts. This volatile atmosphere in their home was a huge burden for Marie and when Jack was offered a place at an ex-forces care home this offered a huge respite for her. Jack refused to go at first, but her persistence paid off and he agreed to give it a try. But, Jack being Jack, he soon came back whinging about their "namby-pamby shit".

Marie had held onto hope that the little time he did manage to stay there would help him, but no such luck existed for them. Jack was soon up to his old games, disappearing on binges before reappearing, terribly worse for the wear, and then disappearing yet again.

Albert, in all his kindness and earnestness to help by offering work, was still a business man. He still needed to provide for himself and his family and so, with huge sympathy for Marie and a heavy (and a very frustrated) heart, Albert was forced to cut his ties with Jack after a very important contract had been lost. Marie sported no ill-feelings, since she understood better than anyone how Jack was an expert at burning bridges and wasting opportunities. So, once again, she was left floating out to sea, with Jack, her anchor, yanking her into the depths. Quite soon, Marie was about to experience the worst week of her life.

UNREASONABLE BEHAVIOUR

It was a sunny summertime afternoon and Millie and Louise were chasing Bo around the garden trying to dress him up in a doll's hat. He would let them catch him and place the hat on his head, then he'd tip it down, the hat falling onto the grass before he gave a friendly bark then began to circle them, tail wagging. Marie stood in the kitchen, smiling at her daughters' antics as she sipped at her tea and enjoyed the short break from her household chores. Then the peace and quiet was shattered.

Beyond the back garden was a narrow lane and suddenly there was Jack, staggering up the street in thoroughly dishevelled state; dirty, unshaven and unhinged and this appearance ended his latest three-day impromptu hiatus from their lives. His steps were uneven and unsteady, interspersed between loud mumblings to himself. Marie caught slivers of his words that came out in a staccato rush, but she could not make sense of them.

Suddenly he made a violent gesture, slashing his hand through the air and bringing it down and with a booming, rage-filled voice that echoed through Marie's head. His mumbling turned into shouting and his unsteady walk turned to an unfocused fury that spiked the air around the house with tension. Instantly, Marie could feel it vibrating in her bones as she put her unfinished tea on the kitchen table.

She had no idea what was going on in Jack's mind, but her list of possibilities did not include playtime and cuddles. Panic began to fill her chest, and she rushed to the back door.

"Millie. Louise," she called to them, her voice coming out in a clipped, rushed way which made their heads snap to attention at the sound of their names.

When they looked up they saw their mother frantically gesturing for them to come into the house. Millie and Louise were smart little girls and they recognized that mum's tone was not one to argue with. With no complaint they were ushered into the house, Bo trailing behind and Marie locked the back door before she took them upstairs and closed the bedroom door.

Almost falling on the stairs as she ran back down and nearly tripping over the rug in the hall, the only plan in mind was to lock Jack out of the house. His entire demeanour and appearance had sent waves of fear coursing through her, alternating between hot and cold and she knew she couldn't trust him around the girls in this state. That's when her luck ran dry.

Jack must have come around the side of the house and he got to the front door just as her hand was on the bolt. He slammed it open, pushing Marie back and she stumbled but caught herself on the hall table. Then she backed slowly into the living room, wanting to coax him to follow her so that hopefully she could ease him into a calmer state.

Jack wasn't going for that and his steps towards her were long, forceful strides. He raised his arms, a movement so quick that Marie could only note that the slight rotation of his shoulders before he shoved her so hard she went flying. There was no saving herself from this and her head smacked into the brick fireplace and she slumped to the ground.

Her vision went dark for a moment and she wasn't sure if she lost consciousness but if she did it was only for a second. A groan vibrated through her throat. She made small movements, testing to make sure her limbs still worked; they did.

Jack had always been a complete sod, ruining Marie's chances at a calm life filled with simple joys. He'd seemed to ruin every chance of happiness as soon as he could... but this physical violence towards her was new and very frightening.

She curled herself into a protective ball as Millie and Louise floated into her dazed mind. What could they be thinking up in their room? Would they come down here? Was Jack also capable of hurting them? These thoughts took a fraction of a second before she was yanked out of them by her hair; Jack held it in his fists as he dragged her across the living room.

He mumbled, loud and angry, a pure jumble of words that only suggested the word psychotic. Now her only thoughts were to get the girls out and it played in her head like a stuck record as Jack went into the kitchen. Still lying on the floor next to the sofa, she heard him opening cupboards and so she gauged the distance between Jack and her; and the distance between her and the stairs. Would she have enough time to get upstairs before he could get back to the living room?

With a move that caused a new jolt of pain in her head, she got to her feet and bolted up the stairs. She retrieved the girls from the bedroom and they could tell by her hushed voice and stricken expression that they should do what mummy told them. They crept halfway downstairs and then stopped as Jack continued to rattle through kitchen drawers. On a mission to find what? Marie was too scared to consider.

"What's daddy doing?" Millie asked, her little voice breaking Marie's heart even more. She gave a quite shush with her finger to her lips as she thought it might make it easier on the girls if they thought this was a game.

"Daddy thought it might be fun to play hide and seek. So we're going to hide, OK? We'll hide so well that it will take daddy hours to find us."

Marie tried to make her voice light like this really was just a game, like the family fun they had in Corfu; that was now light years away. She doubted the girls were buying it, but they were at least playing along.

"I bet if you go to Gabrielle's house next door daddy will spend ages looking for you. He'll be so tired he'll give up and you will win! Do you want to win at hide and seek with daddy?"

"Will he be mad if we do?" a worried Louise asked, thankfully copying her mum's quiet tone. Marie shook her head,

"He knows you're very clever and he's so proud of his clever girls. If he can't find you he'll know he has a pair of very smart girls," Marie assured, "That'll please him to bits." Marie took a deep breath, "Ready?" Both girls gave a solemn nod, suggesting to Marie they were just playing along with this charade, but it would have to be good enough.

Marie willed as little sounds from her steps as possible as she gingerly placed each foot on the remaining stairs, making it to the front door. She turned the handle, easing the door open on its hinges with barely a whisper and ushered the girls out, with Bo hot on their heels. But before she could join them Jack grabbed her, yanking her from the door and slamming it in his daughters' faces before he realised they were outside. Marie screamed with all the power she had in her lungs, "Go to Gabrielle's!"

Jack slammed home the bolt and turned the key before he grabbed Marie's shirt and dragged her across the floor before tossing her onto the sofa. She hit it with a hard whoosh and plop and she could hear the springs grind and the wood frame groan. She was grateful for the soft landing this time, but the jolt again sent spasms of pain crashing through her injured head.

Now he began picking up objects in the living room and smashing them to the ground or onto the walls. The glass vase they had picked up in Corfu, a framed picture of Millie and Louise, and then he picked up a snow globe Grandma Alice gave her one Christmas when she was in primary school. He hurled it at the wall and the glass shattered into fine filaments, spraying the water and glitter so hard she felt droplets on her face. A few pieces of glitter landed on her hand that braced the back of the sofa.

The mismatched lamps on two small tables were swept from their surfaces and crashed to the ground as he continued to ramble incoherently; she knew his PTSD was finally getting the better of him. He picked up a potted plant, a small one given to them by Marie's mother when they moved into their new home, and with a fresh burst of anger hurled it at the fire place. The dark soil and pot fragments dropped to the hearth and carpet. *That could have been my head*, she thought.

Jack continued to grab things with vicious abandon until the living room was littered with his violence and Marie had never witnessed anything like it. Fear constricted her organs and her heart beat fluttered violently. She could feel her skin flush hot and she felt her body brace for an impact she feared might happen but hoped didn't. The uncertainty sent a cold shiver up her spine.

"Jack! Jack!" She yelled his name in repetition in the hope that he would wake from this, "Stop it!" she cried, begging for this nightmare to end.

Suddenly Gabrielle was as at the bay window, banging and yelling for Jack's attention. Marie thought for one moment that he might throw something at her friend, but he simply yanked the curtains closed. Now, almost moving as if in slow motion, he went to stand over her and then produced a long kitchen knife from under his jacket.

Panic and fear shot through Marie's bowels and her attempts to calm him were met with growls and more mumblings. Her thoughts cycled through her daughters and herself; what would happen to them? What would happen to her? How far was Jack going to take this? Then Gabrielle's husband, Martin, tried his hand at calming the situation down.

"Jack mate," came a male voice from the letter box. "What are you doing mate? What's the matter?"

"What? What? What?" Jack yelped like a barking dog.

Martin tried a few more times, but his attempts to coax some reasonable response from

Jack clearly weren't working; he just stood over Marie with the knife shaking in his hand, his eyes piercing her yet seeming to not see her at the same time.

"Hey Jack, why don't you open the door? You and I can go down the road for a pint while the girls clear up and then we'll get the barbecue going. I got some great steaks. What do you say Jack?"

As Martin spent another five minutes trying to convince Jack to open the door, speaking to him in low tones through the letter box, Jack went to sit in the overstuffed chair under the window. With his head bent low and the knife in his hand, he pressed his knuckles to his temple, muttering and mumbling. Then he jumped up from his chair, the springs creaking against their sudden and unexpected release and Marie let out an involuntary scream.

She had been holding her body so tensely, waiting for his next move and his violent moment released a new jolt fear. Here she was, 27 years old and her shitty, anxiety ridden life flashing before her. Jack was quick to grab her and she felt the blade of his knife scratch against the skin of her throat. Then, almost before she realized it, they were at the front door and Jack opened it. He looked at Martin and then, in a calm voice that came with a fleeting moment of lucidity, simply said, "Help me."

Marie was taken aback. What could Martin be thinking as he witnessed this? A drunken, dishevelled man, holding his wife by the hair with a knife at her throat, and the words *help me* coming out of *his* mouth. She didn't have much time to ponder on the absurdity of the moment as the door was once again slammed shut. He continued to hold onto Marie, hair yanked back in one hand, knife blade dangerously close to slicing into her flesh until the police showed up.

Whether it was what Martin had said or lack of understanding by the police, but the seriousness of the situation was severely underestimated and the first car that arrived held only two coppers. There was a solitary siren wail and the flashing blue lights penetrated the closed curtains as a copper pounded on the door. He yelled something Marie didn't quite understand; she thought it sounded something like, "open the door" but something about it wasn't quite right.

Jack, still firmly holding Marie, dragged her over so that he could pound back on the door with the fist that held the knife. Then he took her back to the living room again, her feet crunching over the carpet of broken memories, smashed onto the floor, as she tried to maintain her balance through his erratic moves.

Marie could now hear the voices of men speaking on the front step; they were hushed and had the air of urgency. She recognized Martin's voice but not the others. The letter box flap flipped open and through the doorway she saw a pair of eyes trying to see what was going on. Jack pressed the knife into her throat and his grip tightened. She let out whimper.

"Oh shit!" the voice said, letting the flap fall back down and the sound of metal on metal echoed around the room.

Shortly afterwards the sound of more sirens approached and then Marie could hear the thud of boots and this time it sounded like an army.

Jack was now bracing himself, his body tense and twisting this way and that trying to anticipate an attack from any and all angles. He was bristling and puffing his chest out making guttural noises and Marie was crying.

"Jack, please, think of Millie and Louise, please, don't kill me," she pleaded. "What would they do without a mum or dad? Mum dead and dad in prison. That's not what we want for our daughters."

For the next six hours the police attempted to talk to him through the letter box as he ranted at no one and nothing. He would intermittently hold the knife back at Marie's neck, but sometimes pull away at the sound of her cries. In those grim hours she felt so much heartache for this very seriously ill man—the father of her children. Marie never imagined that her life would be in the hands of a mad man in a hostage situation; let alone that mad man being her husband.

As night descended she desperately hoped that a new act would begin to take shape, but what kind of path was this new script follow? Suddenly she heard whispers from the back of the house and she barely had time to consciously register this before policemen in riot gear came crashing into her home with batons raised. Marie was shoved out of the way as Jack had the knife removed from him in seconds before he was being man-handled out to the back garden.

Marie, concern for her husband still strong inside, shook off the police woman who was holding her and dashed out to where they had dragged Jack. The police had Jack on the ground, and even though he did not resist, they wrenched his arms back and one officer stomped on his ankle. Marie, consumed by her desire to see no more harm done to her family, raged at the copper for being unnecessarily violent towards Jack before she punched him in the face. He stared at her but said and did nothing.

Dragging what would turn out to be a broken leg behind him, Jack was taken through the house and Marie saw that the police had cordoned off the street and the neighbours were all out, full of curiosity, over this long drama; Marie knew it must have felt like they were watching TV. And just like that, it was over as Jack was hauled off in a police van.

A few officers attempted to tidy up Marie's smashed up house as another took her statement. When Millie and Louise were let back into the house she learnt that they had witnessed the police violently taking Jack into custody and for months afterwards they would sleep with unease as nightmares crept into their dreams.

Jack was kept at the police station for two days and it was during that period that Marie knew what her next act would be; she filed for divorce. He was beyond any help Marie could give him. She had herself and two daughters' well-being to look after. It was crystal clear that Jack couldn't be a part of their family unit any longer and she couldn't be the woman who stuck by her man through thick and thin anymore.

The divorce was issued within twelve weeks, citing unreasonable behaviour, which Marie actually found quite funny and somewhat of an understatement. Later, when she and Jack finally spoke, he told her it was the receiving the divorce papers while sitting in jail that hurt most of all. Marie could only shake her head in disbelief.

From there she did her best to carry on as she always had, working at the college, trying to keep sane and raising her girls. And that's when Dave happened. Dave looked after them and cared for them in light of what had happened. But then, Dave was another story completely.

OFF THE RAILS

It was an overcast afternoon when Marie came by for another session. I felt like I was getting some great material for the book, but each story left me amazed about how she came through it all with her humour still intact.

When she arrived she had her hair tied into a loose knot with pieces artfully framing her face. She wore a black skirt that hugged her thighs with short heels that showed off her shapely legs; I just wished I could dress like that.

"Hey you," she said cheerily as I stepped aside to let her in.

"I'm just boiling the kettle. Tea?"

"Oh God please!" she replied, as she followed me into the kitchen. "So how's the book coming along?" It was a couple of weeks since we'd seen each other because her husband had been sick and she'd been too busy. We'd spoken on the phone, but not had any time on the book.

"Great ... I think!" I said filling the tea pot. "I just hope I can do justice to all you've been through. You still don't want to read it?"

"God no!" she laughed as she got mugs out of the cupboard, "I'll still wait 'til it's finished ta."

We took our tea into the living room and settled on the sofa. After a bit of small talk we got going.

"So where were we? OK... after Jack's arrest I managed to carry on and got the divorce and about three months later and I was now with Dave. I kept the house going as long as I could, but really I couldn't afford it."

"Where was Jack at this point? Was he out of jail or what?"

"Out and at it love! I had heard on the grapevine that he'd got out and was shacked up with Debbie again!"

"You're kidding?" I exclaimed.

"No I'm not! I was shocked, but I had no feelings either way about Jack. I was numb and trying my best to just live a normal life."

"So you just tried to ignore it?"

"Yeah, of course. We were divorced and so who he was with was of no interest me other than who might be around the girls."

She paused to finish her tea and I knew she'd carry on with what I needed.

"Anyway, Dave had bought a tiny two bed house the other side of town and offered to take me, the girls and Bo in. I didn't say yes right off, but in the end it was too good an offer, so I sold most of what was left of my furniture and moved in."

"That make things any better?" I asked and she shook her head sadly.

"It was a real struggle in that house. Dave was great at first, but then little signs of stress started to show. He would shout at the kids or the dog for no reason or volunteer for extra shifts at his security job at the college. I knew it was to keep away as opposed to wanting more money, but it was all probably my fault anyway."

"Why's that?"

She looked at me for a moment and then laughed ironically.

"Because I became this paranoid jealous bitch! In hindsight I couldn't blame him cos my behaviour had changed too. I tried to manipulate Dave all the time and this in turn made him really controlling. It was a real disaster of a short lived relationship."

"Sounds like another mess!" I said and she laughed before replying, "Not like me is it?"

"So how long did you and Dave last like that?"

"Nine months. I kept on at the Council and got offered a house back in Bury that I took."

"Would you consider Dave a rebound?" I asked. It seemed curious to me that she would go from such a horrible relationship with Jack and then jump right into a new one after barely any time.

"I never considered that then, but then this was such a low point for me. I probably didn't consider much at all..."

She was quiet as I poured us some more tea from the pot and then carried on.

"The council house was a right shit hole; no heating, and no cooker, we were freezing most of the time. There was not one wall in the house that was decorated. I had never lived anywhere that bad. It was just so bloody dreary and made an already depressing situation that much darker. I wasn't caring for the girls or myself during this period. Jack was back in touch and taking the girls overnight every weekend."

Marie paused to sip from her mug. I was a bit surprised to hear she was letting Jack take the girls but didn't say anything. After her pause she finally said, "I was drinking."

"You mean a lot?" I was surprised to hear that. I knew she liked a drink because we'd certainly seen off a few bottles of wine since we'd known each other, but her drinking then came as a bit of shock. It was hard to believe she would be doing that with her daughters around and after the nightmare they'd been through with their father. She laughed and clearly read my thoughts.

"Yes, can you imagine? The very thing that had ruined my life since I met Jack was now my crutch."

"I guess I was surprised when you first mentioned it, but now I can see how it could have happened. You must have been pretty messed up by all of Jack's crap?"

"Fubbed!" she replied, and when I looked blank she laughed and then added, "Fucked up beyond belief!"

She smiled, but shook her head as she remembered how bad she'd been.

"I was a bloody mess. I lost my job because of my time keeping, kept turning up late because I had huge hangovers all the time and also I started sleeping around so I was shagging half the night as well. I just craved attention from anyone who showed the slightest bit of interest. God I was in a state."

"What about your mum and dad? Weren't they concerned about everything?"

"My brother came to visit one day. He said he had heard from someone that I was in a bad way. He was horrified when he saw what was going on, but I didn't care. Said I was a selfish bitch, but I just wanted to drink and party. He told mum and dad and they came to see what was going on. They stayed fifteen minutes and when I said I was fine they said OK, and left. I didn't see them again for six months."

"You're kidding? They see your awful house and you can't have been a pretty picture if you're brother saw through it, but they just accepted you were OK? Even if they didn't see you being selfish like your brother insisted they should have seen that everything wasn't right."

Marie sighed and picked at her bright painted nail.

"I think they had blinkers on. Jack was out of the picture and they just wanted to believe that everything was better... It was in that crappy house with me a total mess when I lost my best friend..."

"Bo?"

She nodded, tears starting in her eyes.

"That was the last thing I needed right then. It was on a Sunday afternoon and I had taken him and the girls to Heaton Park in Manchester for a walk. All of a sudden he just ran back to the car and was quivering at the door trying to get in. I took them home, but on the way he had what looked like a seizure. I took him to the emergency vet who said he had suffered a stroke. He said he was OK though and might go on another year. So I took him home and settled him down."

"That seems encouraging...?" I suggested, but Marie shook her head as she pulled a tissue out of her bag.

"Within two days he had deteriorated so much, his back legs went and he was wetting himself. I remember sitting on the floor, his head in my lap and he just looked at me with his all-knowing soulful eyes and I knew what he wanted. Debbie looked after the girls and Jack and I took him to the vet."

My eyes widened, "You left your kids with your ex-husband's mistress and went with the man who had held you hostage?"

"Jack had loved Bo too, not as much as me, but he did. Some of our best times, when he wasn't shit faced, were with Bo and the girls. I needed someone who knew how I was feeling so I called him and he came straight round. Oddly enough he was actually sober.

"I will never forget that day. The vet had a radio playing in the background, Radio 2 was on and the song—can you believe it?—'Time to say goodbye' by Sarah Brightman and Andrea Bocelli. That song means so much to me. Every time I hear it I burst into tears because it takes me right back to that surgery floor with my devoted, loving friend's head in my lap, drifting away from me and finally saying goodbye to us. Jack and I were both devastated.

"The timing of Bo's passing enabled me to cry and finally release all of the emotion I had kept held in for years. It was like a tsunami of grief and for days and days, I cried, I missed Bo terribly and I'd lay with my head in his bed, smelling him, clutching his collar."

I wasn't sure what to say, but finally realised and understood why Marie loved him so much. Nobody else had ever really cared about her, but with Bo she'd have had that unconditional love that dogs always give and must have wanted to hang onto that for dear life. She looked at me and I simply nodded my understanding. She smiled and wiped away the tears.

"I'd been in a state before that, but it really was the worst time for me to lose him. I was so out of control during that time and I did some things I'm not proud of.

For instance, one night I left my girls sleeping in their beds and drove to Dave's house; just desperate for companionship, I guess. I'm not sure what I expected to find when I showed up at his place unannounced, but as I drove into his street I saw him walking away from his house with a young girl; they were laughing and carrying on, kissing and hugging, obviously very happy…

"… Well I just flipped Tina. I saw red and was so angry. I revved the car engine so loud he stopped in his tracks, realising it was my car. As soon as I knew he'd recognised me I went for him and luckily he was able to run into a phone box. I pulled back and then for five minutes I kept driving the car up onto the pavement as if to drive into the phone box. I kept revving, shooting forward and then braking as he just cowered. I still can't explain the rage I felt. Whether it was frustration from years of abuse from Jack, or from my uncaring family I don't know, but I have come to realise that when my parents came to that shithole council house I really needed them to believe I was *not* OK despite me trying to convince them that I was… I don't know…."

I said nothing, again feeling sorry for this woman who had become my friend.

"But then I came to my senses and was hit with the realisation of what I was doing, and how terrified Dave actually must have been and how frightened I was of myself. By now he was on the phone, no doubt to the police, so I drove away but didn't go home. I Just sat in a side street, staring out of the window and the police eventually found me and breathalysed me; luckily the test was negative because I'd had a few earlier in the night. They called

Jack to get the girls from the house and I was arrested. I was mortified. I spent two hours in the cells at Rochdale Police station and was let go with a caution. Never saw Dave again or heard from him."

It was kind of ironic that as Marie described yet another rock-bottom point in her troubled life the tape machine stopped. I flipped the tape over to the blank side and looked up at her.

"So what did you do after that?"

"Well, I made a decision the next day. I was going to visit my friends from the telephone exchange in Edinburgh where I had worked all that time ago. I called my old supervisor and, as if by fate, she said there was a job opening in the exchange! It was like a life line. I applied that night. Sent off my CV and was invited for an interview the very next week. It was as if a higher power had thrown me a rubber ring to keep me afloat. I was euphoric!"

"What did the girls think about moving again?"

"Of course I had to think about the girls in all of this. Jack and I had a heart to heart. I could tell he was happy and settled with Debbie. They agreed to look after the girls while I looked for a place in Scotland."

"*What*?" I could hardly believe what I was hearing. "All the stories I've heard about Jack—mean, unfaithful, abusive, alcoholic, unpredictable—and just like that he's settled and you're the angry one with the drink problem who abandons her family?"

As soon as I'd said it I felt bad, but it was such a shock. Then I realised how much in a bad way she'd been. Being her, Marie wasn't angry, but laughed instead.

"That about sums it up. My mum called me selfish, my dad said he couldn't believe what I was thinking, but my inner voice said go for it."

"Was this inner voice on drugs?" I teased. Marie smiled, not answering the question as she stuffed her wet tissue into her bag.

"In hindsight, of course, I know I was incredibly selfish, but I've no idea what might have happened to me if I hadn't got away."

"I can see that now," I replied and had to apologise. "Sorry about my little outburst though, you've shocked me before, but not like that!"

"Oh don't be daft!" she replied, looking at her watch. "You can say sorry with a glass of that Pinot Grigio I know you keep in the fridge!"

"Are you sure you should be drinking?" I asked with a grin as I stood up.

"Vai a prendere la bottiglia e in fretta!" she replied, with a very Italian wave of her hand to shoo me away.

"Well if you want the bottle," I translated, "how about staying for dinner?"

"Let me call the main man!" she replied with a grin. "Can he come too? I doubt the restaurant will be busy tonight and the new manager is coming on well."

"Of course!" I replied. "I've got some chicken and mushrooms so is a creamy pasta alright?"

"Oh lush!"

It was getting on for 5:30 by then and I realised it was getting dark. As she called her husband I got the wine and cooler and two glasses after checking I had enough pasta and then headed back to the living room. I popped some lamps on and poured us both a drink and then she carried on.

"So I got the job and moved up to Kirkliston without my girls, but ready for a new adventure."

"So how were the girls about all this?"

"The girls were actually fine and I'm not sure if they understood in their own little way. Debbie turned out not to be the bitch I'd always thought her to be and I'm still grateful to her for taking on the role of carer to my kids. It must have been hard, but she did actually seem better for Jack than I was."

"So it turned out to be a good move?"

"It sure was. That job was my saving grace and I just loved it because I was back in the bosom of the Army. At first I was living in a barrack block and then my friend's husband was going away on tour for six weeks so she let me move into her spare room; after that I rented a flat. We were working, going to parties on the barracks, loving life!"

"What about the girls I asked?" perhaps still unable to see her leaving them.

"Oh don't worry, I was in constant touch with them and Grandma Alice brought them to visit and they were fine. Pleased to see me, of course, but I could tell they were OK with Debbie. They said their dad was alright as well and I would have known if they were lying."

"What about men then?"

"Gave them up completely," she said with a deadpan face.

"What?" I asked, perhaps a bit loudly and she laughed.

"Of course not! I did have a one night stand once after a party, but I was not sleeping with just anyone anymore. Then a new friend, Christine and I started going out together into the local town. At that time there was a big naval port nearby and there were lots of Army and Navy out on the town every weekend. It was great. Christine and I became very close and did everything together, but she was happily married with two kids and so we just had fun.

"One Friday night we were out on our usual piss up and went to the town's best night club. After getting our usual lager and lime, we made a move towards the dance floor when I spotted a tall, guy looking down at me and smiling. I was smitten. He swept me off my feet and he was to become my saviour, my knight in shining armour and you've met him—his name was John and he's my lovely hubby."

THE MAN OF MY DREAMS

"So that's why you wanted to ask him tonight!" I said with a grin as I stood up. "Let's take a break and I'll get you another glass of wine and start dinner." I glanced down at my watch and asked, "What time do you think John will arrive?"

"Well he said he needed to call into the restaurant so I'd give him about forty-five minutes."

"OK great. I'll get the going with the sauce… I hope I can live up to his standards!"

"Oh that's the chef! John's a good cook, but he's not at that level. If you like, I can help you with the salad?"

"Sure," I said, "as long as we don't chop too loud we can talk some more. Just let me get my tape machine."

Back in the kitchen, I set out all the things for Marie to chop and pulled out my big pot and filled it with water. Before I turned my attention to the sauce I set the tape machine on the counter, checking how much tape was left. I might need another one before the night was out, but I was fine for the time being. Marie sliced tomatoes as I pressed play.

"Tell me what John was like, or how you guys bonded...just, you know, after you were smitten with this tall guy staring down at you."

"Quite frankly that first night was a blur. I only have bits of stuff in my memory because I was pissed as a fart! We danced a bit and then me and John were in the back of his mate's car, his mate and Christine in the front, driving to the car park under the Forth Railway Bridge where Christine had left hers.

"We were canoodling and kissing and John was whispering in my ear a lot; he was pretty shit-faced too. It was a strange sensation because no one had ever done that before. You know, whisper in my ear. I quite liked it! John wrote his phone number down and gave it to Christine because I was so pissed. We said our goodbyes and got out of the car. It was storming like mad out. Violent gusts of wind and as we got near her car Christine stumbled and let go of the slip of paper with John's number on it."

The lettuce and tomatoes now sat in the large wooden bowl I used for salads, and Marie started to shredded carrots and slice cucumber. My eyes were running as I started on an onion, peeling away the skin.

"Oh God! So how did you get in touch with him?" grabbing the tea towel.

"Already I was a little heart broken and in my befuddled state my mind ran through ideas for how I could get in touch with him. There was something about him that seemed different than the others, long-term or one-night stands. Anyway, there was nothing I could do that night, but I went back to the car park in my lunch hour the next day and there was the paper, caught in a bush!"

"Wow! Talk about fate," I said.

"I thought the same thing, maybe not then but at least sometime later. It was 1997 and mobiles were starting to become popular, but I didn't have one, however, telephone boxes were still abundant and one was right around the corner."

"Keep talking," I said as I pulled out a saucepan. "I'm going to start the sauce."

"Oh sure. I called the number and it rang and rang then clicked onto an answering machine. I left a message, something like*: Not sure if you remember me from last night, but it's Marie...erm...I will try later*. I tried five times that day until I finally got John. I was a little worried he might think me a nutter," she laughed.

"I would definitely think you were," I said with a grin.

"You be careful," she said pointing the knife at me, "I have a knife."

I threw my hands in the air as in surrender, "I should know better than to mess with a nutter like you."

Marie laughed then continued her story about John.

"He was charming and lovely and I really hoped it wasn't a put on. He told me he couldn't forget about me and that I was amazing. On the inside I felt 15 again with a million butterflies. Later that evening he picked me up at seven thirty and we went to his house and he cooked for me. I was very impressed.

"Oh is that all it takes? Am I impressing you right now?" I asked, worried in case John was a better cook than she'd made out.

"Not really. You're making me do the salad," she said with that deadpan expression.

"I merely accepted an offer. Oh shit!"

"What is it?" Marie asked, concerned.

"I can't believe I forgot the garlic bread."

"Oh is that all?" Marie gave a nervous laugh, "You had me worried it was something important."

"It bloody well is when you're cooking for a pair of restaurant owners!"

I pulled some uncooked baguettes out of the freezer and stuck them in the microwave to defrost as I made the garlic butter.

"I like to get everything out at the same time. I hate when one thing goes cold when you're still waiting for something else."

"Oh I'm shit at that," Marie laughed. Salad finished, she grabbed her wine glass and took a big sip. "I've been able to perfect drinking wine though!"

"So back to John..." I said, tearing off some pieces of foil.

"Where was I? Oh yeah, dinner. I learnt he was divorced with three kids which he had one night every weekend. He was five years older than me and worked on health and safety for a builder's merchant. He was calm, very attentive and wanted to know all about me. Of course that was a little tricky. I didn't want to tell him *all about me*. I didn't want to scare him off!"

"That makes sense, but I'd imagine you had to tell him some stuff." I said. "Did you explain that you had two daughters and they weren't living with you?"

"Well yes! I did tell him where my two girls were and why. The first thing he said was 'shall we go and see them?' And I just thought, wow he's getting better by the minute. It was around this time my sister Helen got married. Right up to the time of the wedding John kept saying lets go to it but I couldn't face it. After all I had done, leaving my kids with their alcoholic father and beggaring off to Scotland. I just wanted her to have a lovely wedding with no atmospheres! She had a little girl now, our Amy, who I named and I would have loved to have seen her as their flower girl but no, it was best I didn't go. Helen has a boy, Liam as well now. I don't see a lot of Helen but I know she's there if I need her.............but anyway, back to me and John!"

"We spent every spare minute together. Getting to know each other, courting I supposed, doing things as a couple. What I realised was that I'd never done that with anybody before."

I waggled my eyebrows at her, "Yeah? Like what?" I said suggestively.

Marie laughed, "Not like that! Simple things, like cooking dinner together, going shopping, going for a drive, the cinema. Simple, fun, small stuff, but it was really cementing our relationship."

"Well that sounds perfect," I said.

"It felt really...perfect. Life was good and he booked a holiday to Palma Nova. You know, when Majorca was where everyone wanted to go."

"Oh how lovely," I said. "And you felt like you were ready for a holiday together?"

"I was a bit apprehensive, but it was a lovely week together and it was there he says he fell in love with me. He still tells me where we were—it was the Palma Cathedral at night—what I was wearing and that I had a flower in my hair!"

"I wouldn't have pegged John for such a romantic," I said with a grin. "Hang on a sec."

I made sure everything was now going to be done on time and Marie went off to set the table and got another wine glass for John when he joined us. From the corner of my eye I could see Marie take another sip from her wine glass.

"It's fortunate I keep more than one bottle in the fridge. Top up?" I asked, holding up the bottle.

"Oh you're as bad Tina bloody Piper! Look your glass is empty and you've been busy cooking!"

"Yeah, but I only drink so you don't feel like a lush!"

"Piss off!" she said with a grin, squatting herself back down on the stool at the breakfast bar.

"So all was good then?"

"Yeah it was... mostly... but our relationship didn't come without its problems. We had five kids between us for a start."

"That's quite a houseful!" I said.

Marie gave a rueful sigh, "You're telling me!" and at that she took a gulp of her wine.

"But we also had exes that weren't going away any time soon. Unfortunately, Jack had started his drinking again so I had to get the girls. There was no way I was leaving them in that situation. When things were calm and settled between him and Debbie it was ideal, but things with Jack have a way of not really staying calm for long." She gave another sigh.

"So me and the girls moved in with John into his tiny house and his three kids were coming every weekend. My girls started going to a lovely school down the road and they settled well. Made lots of friends and seemed happy for once."

"That doesn't sound too bad..."

"Yes, that part was lovely, but I'm not proud to admit that I started to resent John's kids. There was one girl and two boys and they were close in age to my daughters. I really just had no maternal bond to these children and started dreading the weekends. I was like a child myself. This man was the best thing that had ever happened to me and I wanted him all to myself. His ex-wife made a few waves too—she had left him for another man and married him—like if John and I had plans on a weekend and asked her to keep the kids for one of the nights she would kick up a right bloody fuss. It was just daunting.

"We had lots of arguments during the time we lived at that house. We had very happy times mostly, but some gut wrenching and upsetting ones too... mainly down to my behaviour around his kids...

"Thinking back, I must have made everyone feel very uncomfortable. Having tantrums as an adult woman was really quite shameful, but I guess a lot of it was fallout from all the shit I'd had with Jack and I suppose I was suffering my own PTSD trauma!"

Just then the oven timer dinged and I popped off my stool and pulled the garlic bread out of the oven. I looked at the clock on the wall. It hadn't quite been forty-five minutes, but close. I looked up at Marie.

"Shall we give John a few more minutes before I mix the pasta and sauce and warm it through?"

She glanced at her watch and said, "Just a few. He's usually very punctual."

"That's fine. Carry on then."

"Right... next was another real downer. In 1998 all of us civilians in the telephone exchange got made redundant."

"Oh no! Not your job? I know how much you loved working there."

"I was devastated. I absolutely loved that job. We had no warning at all. Turned up one day for work for the CO, the commanding Officer that is, to tell us the bad news. We were escorted off the camp and that was it. John picked me up. I was a state, but as ever he was fantastic. Telling me not to worry, he said would finance everything and the girls and I would be okay. I felt bad that it had to come to this, but so grateful that I had there to pick me up."

"So did he help you get back on your feet?"

"Yeah he did, but, the same time, my behaviour got worse. I did get another job, on reception at a building society in town. Again a good job and I liked it, but at home in the little house tensions were brewing. I really dreaded every other weekend. I wouldn't even talk to his kids when they arrived. I was childish, sullen, and moody.

"I don't know why, but John was always very patient, he kept plodding on, telling me he loved me no matter what. However, he couldn't keep this up forever and I couldn't blame him. It was the New Year when we decided I should find another place. The girls and I moved into a damp flat only five minutes from John, but far enough away that when he had his kids he wasn't so stressed with me and my behaviour. Though part of me understood, I wasn't happy with the arrangement.

"That six months was shit. I started to do a party plan thing selling naughty knickers and toys at parties to get a bit of extra money in. I met a couple of nice friends doing that- Jan and Kelly. They didn't know each other, I met them at separate parties. Kelly was a single mum so started doing the same as me and our friendship grew and grew. She's still one of my closest friends today. Jan was a good customer of my mine and we started going for Coffees etc. She was very spiritual and was into crystals etc. I missed John even though I saw him most days. So after six months we moved back into Eden Road with him. He made the decision to talk to his ex about having the kids every other weekend. She agreed, but only if we had them for two nights instead of one. John agreed and so we started a life of working, school stuff, and his kids every other weekend, but at least we were having a social life on the weekend we didn't have them and I was doing my parties on the weekends he had had children. We had lots of friends. Christine and I had drifted apart unfortunately, but these things happen. I often wonder what she's doing now."

"God, a funny story about my party plan stuff. When we moved back into Eden Road I had a bag full of demo stuff including little bottles of 'sex pills' that were really sugar sweets- they were just a novelty thing. Passion Pastels they were called. Anyway, Louise took some of these and tried to sell them in the playground at her primary school! Oh my god, that little buggar was selling one of these sugar pills for 5p a time in the bloody school! I found out because the head teacher called me n. I mean I was raging at first- how embarrassing! But when I was telling John he thought this was hilarious and asked Louise how much she had made!"

"Haha, entrepreneurial just like her mother!" I laughed choking on my mouthful of wine. She had such a great way of telling these funny tales about the family.

We were interrupted by the flat's buzzer.

"Must be John," I said. "If you want to let him in I'll finish everything off."

I was just putting the past and sauce into a serving dish when they walked in.

"John, it's so good to see you." I said with a smile as we shook hands.

"I hear my Marie is weaving quite the yarn for you," he said with his lilting Scottish accent.

"Oh you sod," Marie said and smacked his arm. "I speak nothing but the utter truth in all matters. Even the ones that make me look absolutely ugly."

"I can attest to that!" I said with a grin.

"Hey, what did we learn earlier about setting off nutters?" Marie joked.

"You have no knife in your hand now. I feel pretty safe." I said.

Marie laughed, but John mocked concern, "Is there something I should know about? Am I missing all the fun knife fights?"

"No, no," Marie said, "Just an inside joke, pet. No knife wielding here."

"Get your lovely man a glass of wine Marie and then you two go and sit down. I'll bring out the food."

"Oh John'll help—he's a good waiter!" laughed Marie, and we all took the food out together.

"You two ladies know how to show a fella a good time," he said, wine glass in hand as he ogled the sumptuous smelling food.

We enjoyed our meal, chatting about other things; the weather, their business, how the kids were doing.

"John," Marie said, touching his arm. "Do you remember Jan? Her of the Chilli Party?" "Of course I do, I liked Jan!" he said winking at his wife.

"Er.............hold on! What's this? Do I need to start recording?" Sipping on more wine, my head was getting a bit blurry and I said a silent prayer of thankfulness for my tape machine.

"Well, if you want an example of 2 totally naïve idiots ending up at a party they'll never forget then yes!" John said laughing.

I rushed to switch on my machine- this was unusual for John to be so animated and involved in the story telling. I wasn't going to miss this!

"Go ahead" I said to John. "Well," he said mysteriously, "Marie had met Jan doing her sexy parties and Jan really liked Marie..............if you know what I mean? She openly declared she was Bisexual and that Marie was just her type! Anyway to cut a long story short Jan had invited us to dinner at her beautiful house in Glenrothes, which was miles away, to meet her partner Jerry. She insisted we stay the night as a taxi back would have been at least £50. We were looking forward to it and got ourselves ready with an overnight bag. When we arrived Jerry was very nice and got us a large drink each, however he had forgotten, as ordered by Jan to pick up Marie's favourite drink Vodka. So, he and Marie went off in his car to the local off licence and I stayed to help Jan with the Chilli we were to be eating for dinner." Marie started giggling at this point in John's story and was like an excited child waiting for the punchline. The obvious chemistry between these two humans was incredible. I waited for John to carry on. "So, while they were away Jan and I were chatting away about nothing in particular when there was a knock at the door. In came Polly. Polly was a very close friend of Jan's and had been invited for dinner too unbeknown to us. After a very steamy welcome between them, Jan introduced me to Polly. I can honestly say no stranger has ever greeted me like that!" John paused to take a drink looking quite red and flustered. Marie laughed and explained that John was and still is really shy.

"What happened then?" I ventured, dying to know if John had done anything in Marie's absence, although somehow I knew he wouldn't have.

"Jan announced that we should sit in our seats in the dining room ready for Jerry and Marie's return. So, with Jan at the head of the table she told me to sit next to her on one side and for Polly to sit next to me on the same side. Now, to say Polly was ready for anything was a total understatement because when we sat down she started to rub my leg! I did not know what to do. Her hand was stroking my thigh from my knee right up to my crotch. I froze. I've never had any woman do that at a dinner party. Picture it Tina, we are chatting away and this woman who I have never met is making it really obvious what she wants now stroking my balls lightly through my trousers!"

"Oh my god John, what did you do?" Marie and I were laughing more and more with John's reactions as he was narrating this experience.

"Well, I just kept shifting in my chair! After all I didn't want to be rude," he laughed. "Marie and Jerry came back at this point and Marie sat down opposite me noticing my embarrassment, she looked at me puzzled and I just looked down at my crotch and sort of indicated that Polly was touching me there. Jerry was in full flow telling the off licence tail of wrong change or some shite and Polly was interacting as if nothing was happening! It was surreal to say the least. Marie cottoned on but didn't know what to do obviously did you babe?"

"No I didn't" Marie was laughing so much tears were running down her face now. "I didn't want to embarrass anyone by starting on Polly. Neither of us had been in this situation before, but it got a bit fruitier Tina!" she said nudging John to carry on.

"Jesus did it! So, picture the scene now Tina......................I'm sat petrified being touched up by a woman I've never met with my wife sitting opposite. The hosts are carrying on like this happens every day, serving dinner up and chatting away and Marie was just silent................for once! After we had eaten and Jan had served Coffee, Polly had taken off her shoe and her stockinged foot was rubbing the bottom of my leg now. We were talking about Jerry being an ex-policeman when all of a sudden Polly slid off her chair and crawled under the table over to Jan. Because of where I was sat I could see everything that was going on and let's just say there was a lot of slurping!"

Both Marie and I again burst out laughing but John was on a roll now.

"Well, I did not know where to put my face Tina I can tell you! Marie just kept her eyes trained on me and honestly we could have died. Jerry, poured a round of drinks again like nothing is going on. Conversation stopped as Jan started moaning. Jerry invited us to go through to the Livingroom which we gratefully did. Polly and Jan followed and the 3 of them stripped naked right in front of us and started cavorting all over the floor! Marie and I looked at each other and knew we didn't want to be there. We had had far too much to drink and driving home was out of the question. I said I felt sick and pretended to be sick in the loo so that we could go to bed. The last thing I heard Jerry say as Marie and I left that room that night was 'How aesthetically pleasing Polly' looking down at her sucking him off!"

By now I was laughing so hard I couldn't speak! Marie was saying through her hilarious laughing "All true you know!" and "Poor John."

"We didn't know it was a bloody swinger's party!" Laughed John. "I tell you what, I bloody barricaded us into that bedroom and slept with one eye open all night! We left before any of them woke up the next day! Jan and Jerry have split now and he's married to a Thai lady."

Marie started stroking Johns arm as she said "I am still friends with Jan, love her to bits. She's such a lovely person. Live and let live I say!"

"Yes she is" John confirmed. "Very aesthetically pleasing!"

Still giggling at this tale John had so eloquently relayed, Marie and John helped me clear the table and I made some welcome coffee and we adjourned back into the living room. I took the tape machine with me.

"You want to hear Marie at work then John?" I asked.

"What? Spilling the beans on how I dragged her out of the gutter like my own Eliza Doolittle?"

"Yes love. Course you did," said Marie, but her indignation wasn't real and I could see the love in her eyes.

I adjusted the tape machine on the coffee table and grabbed another tape. It wasn't completely filled up but getting too close so I just put a new one in.

"So, do you remember where you were?" I asked Marie.

"Of course because this part is a good part and John came at such a good time. It was summer when he asked me to marry him." At this she paused and flashed John a loving smile.

"Oh I remember this part." John said. "I was there for this. Must've been crackers!"

Marie just gave a small chuckle as she continued.

"We had mobiles now and he texted me to meet him at that same car park we had been at on the night we met-under the Forth Railway Bridge. I thought—this is it! He's had enough of me."

John gasped mockingly, "Never!"

"Oh hush you, the grown-ups are talking! So as I was saying, how wrong I was about John being through with me. I got in his car and he began by asking me three questions: *'Am I the only person you will love for the rest of your life?'* To which I answered, '*absolutely*'. *'Are you ready to spend the rest of our lives together?'* to which I answered, '*yes of course I am*', and *'Would you do me the honour of becoming my wife*? to which I screamed 'YES!'. He put my diamond cluster ring on my finger and we cried."

As she said this she stretched her hand out like a freshly engaged twenty year old, revealing a ring I'd seen many times. It was beautiful and light bounced off the diamonds.

"He had secreted champagne and two beautiful flutes in the car and we celebrated. It was magical."

"I bet." I said. "Such a romantic you are, John," I said and winked at him. He gave me a modest shrug with a proud grin.

"No flirting with my husband now. He's all mine!" Marie said as she threaded her fingers through his.

"When we were ready to leave he asked me to wait half an hour before coming home. Of course I couldn't wait and got back a little too early. He was preparing a little feast for us with candles and romantic music. This man had completely swept me off my feet in the two years we had already spent together. We started talking of weddings and a bigger house. Again life was pretty good. The constant negative was my behaviour around his children."

John let out a little whistle as he said, "Too damned right!"

Marie gave him another playful smack on the arm. "You shush. The grown-ups are still talking."

He looked at her with a smile and stayed quiet as Marie continued, "I just could not bond on any level with them."

"Did you *ever* manage to bond with them?" I asked.

"All of these years later I have done to some degree. I am glad about that, but I still feel pretty horrible for my childish behaviour. Also, money was tight during this time. John was paying his maintenance religiously every month and we had the normal bills to pay. We were trying to set a date for the wedding, but kept having to move it back due to money constraints. I hadn't really been talking to mum and dad since I had left to get my job at the exchange but I didn't need them, life was relatively good and planning for a future with John and the girls was all that mattered to me.

"The date we finally set for our wedding drew closer and at last we were married on July 15th 2000. It was everything we dreamt it would be. Magical and beautiful. My first marriage had been a sham in a registry office with a party back at mum and dad's if you remember. This was the complete opposite. Although it was small all of our friends were there. All of John's family came, but only my brother and his wife and two boys came from my side. When I had told mum and dad the date they booked a holiday instead."

"You what? Their daughter is finally happy and enjoying a magical wedding and they decide on a holiday somewhere else?" I asked, incredulous.

Marie shrugged. "A true measure of what I thought meant to them."

"That's down right... it's just despicable!"

"It was what it was," she said with a shrug. "The weather was rainy and windy for three whole weeks leading up to the wedding. I was a nervous wreck worrying how it would be on the big day but all we had that day was glorious sunshine. My girls and John's daughter were my bridesmaids and my friend Mary was my maid of honour. Her husband was John's best man and his two boys were ushers.

"My dress was a medieval style three-piece gold and ivory dress. I adored it. I still have it in fact. When I arrived at the hotel with my brother, who was giving me away, I found that the room in which we were to be married had been set up like medieval woodland with logs tied together with ivy at the end of each row of chairs and the ceiling was draped in a beautiful organza. It was my very creative friend Jeanette who had secretly done this for us. She had even made table runners for the signing of the register with special chair covers that had our initials on them. It was so beautiful."

"Sounds amazing," I said remembering my own 'quickie' in a registry office followed by lunch in a steak house.

Marie nodded, "Yes, it was. It was just so perfect for me. During the ceremony when John was saying his vows he was very emotional and had to stop speaking for a few moments to gather himself. It was so lovely."

At this point he grabbed a tissue from the box on the coffee table and dabbed at his eyes as if blubbering. This earned him another clout before Marie drank some coffee and then continued.

"We had a fantastic reception with a real party atmosphere and people still talk about our wedding to this day. When we went up to our room in the hotel my brother and the best man Gav had been in and turned *everything* upside down! No doubt they thought it was hilarious, but we were not very amused."

"We spent so much time switching everything back when I really only had one thing on my mind," John said and I started laughing.

"Oh you poor darling!" I said

"It wasn't a one-way street you know!" Marie corrected me. "Of course when it was all sorted out I only had sleep on my mind!"

"That's not how I remember it," suggested John and Marie laughed raucously before adding:

"So we started married life together on the back of such a beautiful wedding day. I had the man of my dreams at last and finally my girls and I were settled. What could go wrong in my life now I asked myself?"

MORE UPS AND DOWNS

"The way you say that it has an air of ominous foreboding about it." I suggested.

Marie shrugged, "Life is life. It only keeps doing what it does."

"I suppose that's one way of putting it," John said with a half shrug and a swig of his coffee. Marie and John exchanged knowing looks, but I had a hard time imaging more bad things could befall them after such a lovely marriage ceremony.

"But things didn't start going bad straight away. After the wedding we decided we'd get a bigger house. We really needed the room with the kids and everything appeared to be going pretty well. John put his little two up two down on the market and we began to look for our next home."

"Were you working then?" I asked.

"I was." Marie said with a bit of a pause, "I had several part time jobs. One was for a loan repayment company and oh, it was awful. These poor people were already so hard up and couldn't afford to repay their loans. Then I was a receptionist at a hotel. I was not fond of any of it and had a hard time coping with these menial jobs. I knew I wanted something more. That's when our gift shop, Inspirations, was born."

"Tell me more..."

"We'd go to Glasgow and buy all sorts of crap; framed pictures of dolphins, ornaments, kid's toys, scarves, jewellery and so on. Real tat but it sold like mad."

"People love their cheap crap," agreed John and Marie gave him a little slap on the thigh, "Hey, only I get to call it crap."

"People love inexpensive sparkling jewels," John rephrased to appease Marie.

"Yes" she said with a bright smile towards her husband. "And I suppose due to the rack of earrings by the till we had quite a few folks inquire about piercings. That's where next money making idea came from."

"You started piercing ears?" I asked and she nodded.

"Of course, I didn't offer piercings at the time, but it really got me thinking. After some research I found a company that sold a kit and offered training. Sharon was my trainer and what a lovely lady she was. It became a popular service and I had a ton of bookings."

"So all was still going well?"

"It was... and then it wasn't. It was also around this time I was finally able to have my hysterectomy. I'd been wanting for ages, having really suffered through my periods and my PMT made Frankenstein look like a pussy cat. That meant John and the kids and to bear the brunt of it and suffer as much as I was."

"So no kids for you and John then?" I suggested and John shook his head.

"It was never on the radar" she said.

"Nope," John agreed, "Five between the two of us seemed plenty and I just wanted to enjoy Marie and our time together." John put his hand on Marie's thigh and she gave him a loving smile.

"After a failed marriage each we just wanted to work on making ours successful." Marie placed her hand on top of John's.

"I would say you guys had the right approach." I said.

"Some might say it's selfish but I say so what?! It's our marriage." Marie said.

"Too right." I said.

"So early in 2001 I had my operation and that's when things began to go wrong. It wasn't the operation that was the problem, it turned out I had a severe sensitivity to morphine. While still under from the anaesthetic I began to vomit and then it just carried on. John was worried sick—God what a terrible pun—but was told by the nurses that it was normal even though I still kept vomiting in my sleep.

"I was still out of it so I don't remember this, but then John notified the nurses that I was also beginning to swell all over rather quickly. Now they were worried and so I was rushed out to a side room where they had to flush all the morphine out of my system. My body had started the process of shutting down!"

"I had never been so scared. I thought I might lose her for a while there." John said, still looking like it bothered him.

"It was bloody awful Tina. At the time I was in so much pain but I had to wait for the morphine to leave my system completely before they could give me anything else. In the end I was in the hospital for three weeks and the pain was unbearable. Even soddin' childbirth had nothing on that!"

"That must have been awful," I said as grabbed the pot and freshened our coffee. "So after the hospital you went home to finish recovering?" I added.

"I knew I had to recover quickly," Marie said after she took a gulp of her fresh coffee. She leaned back after setting it down on the table.

"The gift shop wasn't going to run itself and after six weeks I reopened the shop. Boy had we been missed and we did loads of business in the spring and summer of that year. In addition to ear piercing I started to get requests for nose and other piercings. I had Sharon back in to train me in nose piercing—I was obsessed and I loved it.

"I built up a good reputation for being calming with people, especially young girls and for doing clean and healthy piercings. After some more research I decided I'd rather do body piercings so my little gift shop morphed into a body piercing studio. I went on to do some more training in Accrington with a lady called Yvonne. She did all sorts of piercing, tattooing and other beauty stuff."

"That has to be one of the most interesting business shifts I've ever heard of—from selling crap to making holes in people!"

"Cheeky cow! I suppose it is," Marie said with a laugh. "But it was so much fun." She leaned back and crossed her legs then placed a stray hair behind her ear. "We'd outgrown the gift shop space so I found a new place in the heart of town. The business grew as did my good reputation. I rented out space to a tattooist and we were both really busy. People loved their body mods!"

John gave a small laugh and I glanced over at him, "Ever let her pierce anything on you?" I asked.

"Oh God no! I would never let her near me with her scary tools!"

"So at this point business was good..."

"I see a pattern emerging," I interrupted and Marie nodded then continued, "So with my having learned how to pierce everything from the navel upward—no naughty bits for me—I trained another piercer and the tattooist's girlfriend came on board too. We had the space to do it and business was good so John and I decided to book a holiday in Florida with my girls."

"That sounds lovely but there was a snag?"

"Oh yes," said John and his voice had changed to a mournful tone. "My dad."

"We'd just sold the house and got a three bedroom semi and all the paperwork, the meetings and the moving was exhausting. Then John's dad fell ill with really aggressive throat cancer."

Marie's face was twisted as the memory of her father-in-law filled her mind. "The last time I saw him was at his house. He was lying on the couch and just ever so thin. He'd lost so much weight and when he tried to get up I told him to stay where he was. He began to sing 'always look on the bright side of life.' It was...heart wrenching."

I watched John's face; he looked down, saddened by the memory of his sick father. I looked back to Marie and listened as she continued.

"It was a dark time for the two of us. His dad died in hospital. The funeral was a sad affair with tears all around. It made me think of my parents and our relationship and how shit it was. Despite my success with marriage and my business we still weren't talking."

"I miss my dad but I'm glad we had a good relationship. I wish Marie could have had better parents. It makes me angry and sad when I think about," said John and I never heard him speak so bitterly.

Marie gave John a sweet smile, "Thanks, honey. But I just expect it will be like this forever with them" she said with a slight shrug. "But at this point the Florida holiday was coming up. We thought it would be best to cancel it, but John's family all said to go. I wasn't so sure but we eventually decided we should take the trip and I trusted the studio in the hands of the tattooist and the other two employees.

"We had a lovely time, but I was still not completely recovered from the hysterectomy and was tired in Florida. John did all sorts of things with the girls while I chilled out at the resort. I called the studio and while they were telling me everything was fine I just had an awful feeling that something wasn't quite right."

"The girlfriend..." said John and Marie nodded her confirmation, "The girlfriend........ and she was the worst. While I was away this woman set out to destroy me."

I was taken aback, "That's a bit dramatic."

"I should have trusted my gut." Marie said more to herself than me. She glanced down shaking her head then back up at me.

"As soon as we left for Florida this woman's mission was to destroy my reputation and turn my staff against me. So yes, it was dramatic."

"What did she do?"

"For starters she started telling all my clients how bad I was at piercing and they should go to someone else. She also called Yvonne the trainer and told her all of my business plans, that I was training people and that she should prosecute me. I still have no idea what for. But all of this unravelled after the Florida trip."

"That's awful. What did she have against you?"

Marie shrugged, "She just wasn't happy with her lot in life, she wanted to take what I had. Maybe because she thought she could take it for herself. I'm not sure. When we arrived back home I really wanted to phone up the shop to make sure everything was OK. The girlfriend answered and said to me, "You had better get the fuck down here and answer some questions." I was just stunned, my stomach was doing summersaults and I wondered what I had to answer for. Me and John went straight to the studio."

I grabbed my coffee for a sip and listened as she continued.

"Once at the studio we were greeted by a right mess; no stock in the cabinets, stone faced employees, and the tattooist in the middle of a tattoo. The girlfriend wanted to know why I was teaching other salons to pierce. How ridiculous is that? Training was part of my business in the same way that Yvonne trained me. I was gobsmacked. I thought she must be joking but she wasn't. It had to have been jealousy. After a row in which she was completely irrational she ordered the tattooist and the other piercer to leave with her. John and I were absolutely in shock. And so was the tattooists' client! He was half way through his tattoo and we had to give that guy money to get him to leave with a half-finished tattoo. After they had gone we checked everything and discovered an empty till, hardly any stock and a dirty studio. We called the police who did nothing. Just said it was a domestic situation!"

"That is insane. How can your employee steal your stock and the money from the till and the police tell you it's domestic?"

"Lazy coppers." John spat, "They just didn't want to have to deal with anything about it."

Marie nodded. "As the weeks went by after this attack on us I had a hard time sleeping. I withdrew and wasn't coping well. We were still busy even though they had slagged me off all over town. Word had spread about what had happened and I got a call from another tattoo artist who offered his services. I agreed. Then came a lady who wanted to learn how to pierce and work in the studio. So I started again, tried to build my reputation back up, but my trust was shot to pieces."

"I bet that was hard." I was beginning to feel like a psychologist, but I didn't mind. I never found her stories anything but fascinating and surprising.

"It was so hard. Not being able to trust anyone is a tough way to run a business." She grabbed her coffee and took a gulp. "Now it was time to have serious problems with Louise."

"Oh God, what now?"

"She was becoming very unruly and I took her to the doctor who referred her to a specialist in child mental health. We had several meetings with this woman who I disliked intensely. She always had this air about her that made me believe she blamed me for Louise's behaviour, which got worse. She would do really awful stuff like pour bleach into Millie's fish tank. She threw a TV out of the window, stole money, and was drunk at school. The worst one was when she accused me of battering her every night. The bloody police and social work department were involved in that one. They knew it was made up but by God I *could* have battered her that day."

"That girl was a right mess," John said.

"Why was she behaving so badly then? Did they diagnose anything?"

"That specialist said she had Reactive Attachment Disorder—RAD. We had never heard of it, but she explained that while Louise was in my womb I was under extreme anxiety with her dad. As a result I didn't bond with her when she was born because all of my focus was on Jack. Although I was a practical mum and kept Louise fed and cleaned and dressed nice, I was not an emotional one. I wasn't there with hugs and kisses and talking about feelings."

"She's different these days," John noted.

Marie sighed, "Did Louise no good then."

"But you're a good mum. You shouldn't be so hard on yourself." John grabbed Marie's hand and gave the back of it a little reassuring kiss.

"Thanks honey."

"What happened after the diagnoses?"

"I was angry because it was all directed at me. I didn't have the tools to nurture Louise because of my own childhood experiences and then I'd gone straight into a loveless marriage.

"So we had to adapt to trying to live with this. It was really hard. Her off-the-wall behaviour was draining and Millie was suffering too as all of our energy was on Louise. I was still resenting John's kids. Why was my daughter out of control yet his kids seemed normal? None of it seemed fair."

"And then I lost interest in the studio and decided to leave Ian the tattooist to it. My behaviour became a bit erratic, going out a lot, going away for the weekend when John's kids were there and leaving him with all five. I was spiralling downwards and didn't know what to do next. I needed to earn money but wasn't sure how. Then we met David and Fi, the friends of a friend..."

She stopped and glanced at the clock and it was almost 11:30."

"Oh God, look at the time. We'll have to stop there Tina and get home. If I start on the next bit we'll be up all night."

"No problem and thanks so much both of you, that's been great," I said as I stood up disappointed that they were having to leave. "So what have I go to look forward to next? Not more problems I hope!"

"The Dungeon Master and the Mistress! Now that *is* going to be interesting," she said with a twinkle in her eye as she grabbed John's hand.

DUNGEON MASTER AND MISTRESS

"Who is that? That bloke looks dead dodgy!"

Marie sat in the passenger seat of their car next to John. It was late afternoon and the grey clouds covered the sun. A man had walked up to the building they were staking out and she had grabbed John's forearm.

"He's just a regular guy. Relax," replied John, trying to reassure Marie while he sought to release the grip of her newly painted bright red nails.

"Oh bloody hell....... He's going in. He's a customer! Oh shit! Do they all look as shifty?"

The building was grey with a flat roof. The outside was bland and didn't speak of what might be hiding inside.

"Just relax hen. We need the money. You said you were up fer it," John reminded her, and then saw the look on her face. Now he put his hand gently on her forearm. "You can back out. We don't really know them all that well."

"No. No. I think this is fine. We can do this."

"We?" John questioned as he quirked his eyebrow at her.

"I... I can do this."

"Remember what David said? He's always there and you'll be perfectly safe."

"Right. Right." she replied, but she sounded unconvincing. Her voice quivered slightly as her nerves continued to get the best of her.

"Ready?" John tapped Marie's hand affectionately as she continued to stare at the building as if it would reveal some great secret.

"Hmm?" she said absent mindedly.

"Marie?"

"What?" She turned her head to her husband.

"Are you ready?" he asked again.

"Oh. Yes. I mean no... but yes. Oh fuck it! Let's go."

John got out of the driver's side and was heading across the pavement when he noticed that, despite her bravado, Marie still hadn't budged. He walked around to her door and pulled it open. She got out without a word and joined him as they headed towards the front door of the building.

Fi opened the door after they buzzed. She was a petite woman in her late 30's with bottle red hair, but her large bust was squeezed up and out of her latex corset that she wore with a matching, tight and very short skirt. She greeted them with a smile that seemed more appropriate for meeting up in aisles at Tesco—quiet incongruous with her clothing.

"Hello!" she said cheerily and stepped aside to let them through. "I was a little afraid you might not show."

They walked into an expansive waiting room with plastic chairs and a plain wooden coffee table.

"I wouldn't do that to you guys" replied Marie, thinking that was just what she wished she'd done.

"Welcome to our humble dungeon."

The voice startled Marie, and she spun around to see David who had just stepped out of a door in the back of the room. His gaze was intense as he stared into Marie's eyes.

"Thank you," John said, also now wishing he wasn't there.

"I have to go work with a client now," Fi said. "If you'll excuse me, David can show you around."

"OK," Marie nodded.

David walked behind the receptionist's desk and pulled out a manila envelope.

"The pictures Fi took of you been developed," he said as he set the eight by ten photos on the desk and spread them out.

"Well look at you, babe! Wow!" drooled John as he leaned over the desk and closely perused the photos.

"Not bad. But those..." Marie pointed to the photos showing her face, "aren't going to be on the website are they?"

"Not if you would prefer they didn't," David replied, segregating the ones that only focused on Marie's body, dressed in a black corset, suspenders and stockings and thigh length boots.

"If you approve of these we'll get them up ASAP."

Marie glanced at them again and then gave a small nod of her head.

"Nervous?" David asked.

"It's all just so new to me," admitted Marie.

"I think you'll end up really enjoying your time here. Let's look around shall we?"

John and Marie had met David and Fi through mutual friends. At first they seemed just another ordinary couple, but then they learnt that they were a master and mistress of a dungeon. When the conversation had suggested that John and Marie could do with some extra cash, both David and Fi were convinced that Marie would make an excellent mistress. Marie posed for some pictures wearing some of Fi's clothes; they had been a bit small and hard to get into, but the resulting pictures had certainly excited John.

David stepped from behind the desk and walked to one of the doors off the reception area, and they entered a narrow hallway.

"Fi is in that room," he said quietly, pointing to the first door on the right. "When she's done I can show you in there."

They went into the next one and it was set up like a classroom. Marie thought that, minus the sex instruments on the teacher's desk—canes, leather floggers, restraints—it almost looked like it belonged in a school. There were students' desks and a black board with random writing all over it. In the back corner was a stool with a dunce cap.

Once more, Marie wondered what she was letting herself in for, but then reminded herself that she and John needed the money. Making light of it she laughed and said, "Right lads! Which one of you wants to put on the dunce cap?"

She was really intrigued by the prospect of being a dominatrix. Shame she couldn't have Jack as a subject, she thought as she grinned to herself momentarily.

"Fi holds sessions with five to six guys in here once a week," David said, breaking her reverie.

"Really?" John asked, but Marie felt it was more out of politeness. John looked distinctly uncomfortable now and she knew there was no way 'school' would be played out at home!

"They like the classroom experience. Punishment for being disruptive, being humiliated in front of a classroom, being sent to the back to wear the dunce cap."

Marie ran her hand over the instruments of torture on the desk, but didn't actually touch anything. "Interesting," she said for want of nothing better to say. Inside she was shitting herself.

"Don't worry," David said with a grin, "We wouldn't start you with something nearly as intensive as a classroom full!"

"But later you can be a teacher like you always dreamed of being," John teased.

Marie gave him a light swat on her arm.

"I never imagined being a teacher in a room like this!"

They went to the next room and David opened the door. Inside was an adult sized baby nursery. There was a play pen, a high chair, baby gowns, nappies—all adult sized. Marie was gobsmacked. She knew of adult babies, but this was something else.

"Each to their own" she said with a smirk.

"Yes..................each to their own with a price tag of £300 per session for adult baby!" David laughed. "Oh my god! You have to be kidding me" Marie was that shocked she sat down on one of the desks.

On the other side of the room was a man wearing black leather shorts and a black leather mask.

His flesh was freckled and slightly reddened in places. Probably around 30, he was covered in hair, but it wasn't all that thick. He was filling adult sized bottles with milk.

"This is Sally. He's our slave," David introduced them. "This is Marie and John. Marie is going to be our new dominatrix. John is her husband."

There was a pause as, head slightly bowed, Sally stared at them through the eye holes in his leather mask, half-filled bottle in hand.

"You may speak, Slave."

"Oh my actual God" thought Marie, this is ridiculous!

"Nice to meet you. I'm Sally. I do all the cooking, cleaning, act as footstool for mistresses tired legs................and anything else that might be required of me around here." His voice was masculine, but with a slightly high affect, like he was trying to sound more feminine.

Over compensating for her husband's embarrassment Marie piped up "Oh Sally, I hope you won't be exclusive and will act as footstool for me!"

Immediately the air changed in the room. Sally glanced at his Master and with one look from David he scuttled away back to his bottled filling. "I would ask that you don't give Sally any choices. He is here to be TOLD what to do, not to decide..........." chided David and turned to leave the classroom. John looked at Marie and slapped the back of his own hand rolling his eyes. "All very serious!" he whispered. The two of them followed David stifling giggles.....................just like school kids.

Marie turned slightly away from John and David back in the reception area, pretending to scan the room. She had felt a fit of giggles bubbling up inside and didn't want to let it out. As she was managing to get herself under control David continued.

"Sally is an excellent slave. He enjoys pain. We like to flog him occasionally. A treat for a job well done. Isn't that right?" David looked at Sally as he entered reception and Sally averted his eyes.

"Yes, Master," Sally said in agreement.

"Sally, wait. I think Mistress may be done with her client."

Fi walked her client to the main door back out onto the street. The front door was closing and Fi made her way to the desk.

"Hey! How was the tour?"

Marie cleared her throat, "En... enlightening." She wondered where that stammer had come from.

"In a good way I hope?" Fi asked.

"Oh yes," John said, with an encouraging grip of Marie's hand.

"There's still the main chamber. Let's enter, shall we?" David walked over to the door closest to the reception desk. Marie wondered why he had to talk so posh about it. And why was he so serious all time?

The main chamber was more decadent than the theme rooms. The floor was a shiny black, and three of the walls were also painted in the same colour, with the fourth a rich red. An elaborate chandelier hung from the black ceiling, and there were black chairs and couches all littered with red velvet cushions. There was a pommel horse looking contraption in the centre with straps all over it. There was a large X frame on the wall covered in straps, and to the right of the door was a glass cabinet filled with various accoutrements of the trade: whips, flogs, dildos, lube, chains, and toys. Marie stifled a shiver.

"John, why don't you let me whip you a little?" Fi suggested.

John made shocked eye contact with Marie. Then the look changed to panic and he signalled, "get me out of here!"

"Yeah, I think that's a great idea!" Marie said with a wicked grin, and John now flashed her look. "Well! I do need to learn my technic"

"Just through your jeans," added Fi with an encouraging smile.

"Uh, OK," John acquiesced, but he still looked distinctly uncomfortable and Marie knew she'd pay for it later.

John nervously walked up to the pommel horse and laid face down across it and, with a little nervous laugh said, "Like this?" He leaned over it a little and put his hands on the other side.

"Stay just like that," Fi said.

She grabbed a cat o' nine tails and stepped a couple feet back. She swished the leather straps in the air and snapped it over his jeans covered bum. Marie couldn't help but give a little giggle, and David even gave a small chuckle. Fi did it a few more times and said, "Not so bad, huh?" she asked as John stood up, relief all over his face.

"Not nearly as intense as when Marie gets going in the bedroom!" he replied, and Marie's cheeks bloomed a rosy red.

"There is definitely an art to it," David assured.

"Yeah?" Marie asked.

"We'll have you work with Sally to perfect your technique."

Over the following few days, Marie came back to begin work with Sally. Initially she borrowed Fi's clothes, but had to purchase her own. It was a black corset that cinched her waist into an hour glass figure and latex boots that hit her mid-thigh. She never said anything even to John, but Marie felt absolutely amazing in her outfit. She was looking forward to her next purchase after working with a few clients.

The work with Sally was slow going. He did a good job instructing her how to whip him, but sometimes she was too light and other times Sally had to cry for mercy. Marie worked hard to find that sweet spot of pleasurable pain. After several sessions, David told Marie he thought she was ready for a real client. The interest from her website photos was growing and David didn't want to hold Marie back any longer.

A week after that first visit it was the big day, and Marie almost asked John to join her. Not in the chamber, of course, but just to the dungeon. But once she got there she was actually excited at the idea of putting into practice everything she'd been learning on a real client, and not just Sally the Slave. She stood in front of the floor length mirror in the dressing room and gazed at herself. Who was this sexy dominatrix staring back at her?

With the thigh high boots and the black leather corset, Fi had done her make up for her and it was wild with black smoky eyes and deep red lips. Her face matched the main chamber. Under all that make-up, latex and nerves she actually felt powerful, like an Amazonian goddess. She replayed the routine in her mind, and the first thing she was to say to the client was to set the ground rules for their session:

1. No looking me in the eye
2. Stay three feet away at all times
3. No touching

4. No crying out in pain unless you have permission
5. No touching yourself or orgasming unless you have permission

She didn't consider herself a prude, but she couldn't imagine what her face looked like when Fi told her the last rule. They can orgasm during this? But now Marie considered it part of her power over them. Working with Sally she didn't feel empowered or the slightest bit turned on, but now she wondered how she'd feel once in the room.

"Michael's here," Fi said as she poked her head behind the black curtain that covered the dressing area. "Are you ready to meet your first client?"

Marie nodded and followed Fi to the reception area. She walked confidently in her extra high heels. She'd spent hours practicing so she wouldn't look......or feel stupid.

"Michael, this is Mistress Mary," Fi said as she introduced the two. Marie hadn't known what her name was going to be after the word Mistress and she was dying to burst out laughing! Mistress Mary? Mistress fucking................................Mary? So underwhelming! Michael stood from one of the plastic chairs and shook Marie's hand. "You're going to be her first client, how do you feel about that?"

"Whoa, that's kind of exciting." Michael said, the words sounding very strange coming from someone who looked like a 40 year old accountant. "I usually see Fi so it should be interesting to..." He trailed off and looked over Marie from toe to fake eye lashes. "You're very sexy Mistress Mary."

"Thank you," Marie said, suddenly feeling a bit shy.

"Sally!" Fi called, and when the slave walked in he was instructed to get Michael ready and Sally whisked her first client away.

"Go ahead," Fi patted Marie on the bum, urging her towards the main chamber. Marie gave a little jump and headed into the room. As Fi closed the door behind her she gave Marie a wink.

Sally was helping Michael remove all his clothes. Once naked they were able to officially start the session, and Marie sought to get herself into role.

"Go sit on the sissy stool!"

He obliged instantly.

"Face the wall." She said when he sat with his knees together, his eyes on her.

Marie recited the rules to him and when she was done she said, "Do you understand? Answer me."

"Yes, Mistress. I understand." Michael was timid but enthusiastic in his response.

Marie was beginning to feel the part of a dominatrix a little more as Michael took on the role of the submissive slave. She glanced over at Sally who gave a slight, approving nod.

"Now get on your hands and knees and crawl to the pommel horse."

Michael kneeled off the stool and onto the ground.

"Slowly."

Sally grabbed a whip and handed it to Marie.

"Sally, tie him to the horse," she ordered as she smacked the whip in her hand and took a step back. "Take your time."

"Thank you, Mistress," Michael said. He was trying to look submissive, but could not hide the excitement and anticipation in his eyes.

Once Michael was completely strapped in, Marie began to lightly tap his flesh with the tip of her whip. She smacked him harder and moved the whip from his shoulders to his rear, to the back of his thighs and the bottom of his feet. Michael was clearly into being whipped, but his safe word was 'sore'. Marie was sure he wasn't going to need it. She couldn't imagine hitting him so hard that he couldn't take it.

The session went on and she swapped to the cat o' nine tails. She swished it in the air, like Fi had done that first day when hitting John over his jeans. Then she smacked him in the middle of his back, swished it in the air and then smacked him hard across the cheeks of his bum. She was glad he was facing away from her because she gave a little flinch at the sound of the crack on his skin. She hit him on both places again, and his back was now covered in red welts, but she still didn't hear 'sore' yelled out. All he kept uttering was "Thank you, Mistress" over and over again.

Normally very polite, Marie had to hold back from saying 'You're welcome," and she also struggled to keep back the giggles. Now she was actively involved with a client, she couldn't believe the ridiculous situation she had gotten herself into, but she was still a bit nervous as well. Am I doing this right? She thought to herself. He seemed be enjoying it, so she carried on.

There was a clock over the door, Marie glanced at it and noted there was only 5 minutes left.

"Sally, give me the whip," she ordered and grabbed it out of his hand. Michael was still begging for more whippings.

"Yes, Mistress Mary, please! I deserve the punishment. Hit me harder!" he whimpered.

Marie took the whip and started smacking his skin with hard whacks, cracking the whip through the air. One after the other, she realised she'd become desensitized to the feeling of hitting someone so hard. She heard Michael whimpering some more, until finally she realized he was yelling a word.

"Sore! Sore!" he was yelling and she stopped immediately, the feeling of empowerment being replaced by an awful sinking feeling in her stomach. How many times had he uttered 'sore' before she heard him?

Sally untied him and, unable to look at him, Marie walked out of the chamber. She inhaled sharply as she stepped into the cool air of the reception area.

A few minutes later Michael popped out, looking a little worse for the wear, but wearing a grin along with his suit and tie.

"Thank you, thank you, thank you Mistress Mary. That was amazing," he said as he paid for the service and then walked out the door.

"Well?" Fi asked as she too the dungeon's cut and handed Marie the rest of the money.

"Oh God! I thought he was going to be so upset. He had to yell his safe word!"

"Well, hon, there's a safe word for a reason. Ready for your next client?" Fi looked at her booking schedule. "Rick, a ballbuster, 14th at 2:30?"

Marie said a silent prayer to herself and with a giant smile said, "Sure, absolutely."

It was a few days later and Marie was dressed and ready for her next appointment. She walked out into the receiving area and David was there with the new guy.

"Mistress Mary," David said, "Meet Rick."

"Hello," Marie said and extended her hand for a shake. Do you shake new client's hands? She wondered.

"Wow, look at you!"

An overweight and bald guy in his fifties, Rick did the same thing Michael had done, and slowly look her up and down, not worrying about where his eyes lingered.

"Rick, can you tell Mistress Mary what kind of experience you'd like?"

Rick wasn't shy about explaining to Marie that he was into ball busting. Marie already understood from David and Fi what that meant, but she had to work a little harder to get Rick to explain more in depth what exactly he wanted to happen in the chamber.

Once in the room, she told him to lie across the pommel horse which he did so, with his penis tucked in and his balls exposed. Marie reached into the cabinet and pulled out a mask, which Sally put on before tied up Rick. Next, she grabbed a feather duster and tickled his balls. He squirmed against his restraints and let out a noise akin to a stifled giggle.

She had already recited the rules to him, but reminded him again.

"Do not make any noise!" Marie instructed.

"What are you going to do to me if I do?" Rick tested.

Marie grabbed a ruler and handed it to Sally.

"Smack him."

Sally took the ruler and smacked it against Rick's balls.

"Oh yes!" Rick moaned and Sally did it again as Marie demanded he be quiet.

After the slapping of his testicles with the ruler a few more times, Sally grabbed a rubber band and pinged it against Rick's balls. She felt somewhat relieved that the Slave was doing a lot of the work, but Rick would soon be expecting the stronger stuff.

Marie and Sally made eye contact, and with a submissive bow of his head, the Slave moved to the sissy stool and faced the wall. Marie felt a little lurch in her stomach as she worked up the nerve to do the next part. Trying to think of herself as goalie kicking a ball up the pitch, she took a couple of steps and then slammed her thigh high boot into Rick's balls. He let out an agonised scream.

"Oh my god!" Marie shrieked and immediately ran to pull his mask off. "Are you all right?"

"Oh for fucks sake!" Rick shouted, clearly pissed off that she had ruined an otherwise stellar experience.

"Blue," Sally said, and she looked puzzled. "That's his safe word. You had forgotten to ask him," he added before he made a hand gesture for her to get out of the room.

Marie was just explaining to David and Fi in the reception area when, a few minutes later, Rick stormed out of the chamber.

"You got a real lame girl here!" he said to David and Fi. "Don't expect me to pay for that...................... rubbish!"

"Of course not, sir," David said, and Rick bolted out the door, his suit jacket in hand. Marie looked up at David and Fi from one of the plastic chairs.

"Maybe this isn't the thing for me?" "No, I think you may be too sub!" said David.

It was actually quite funny.................... imagine this guy expecting THAT experience and the woman inflicting this pleasure stopping with her character of mistress to ask if you are ok? Needless to say that's where Marie's career in the world of dungeons ended!

TRIALS AND TRIBULATIONS

It was quiet as I sipped my drink, waiting for Marie to arrive. We'd agreed to meet at a wine bar between where we lived for happy hour drinks and, because it was still quite early, there were just a few other people sitting at scattered tables. There were bits of conversations, but they were indecipherable mumbles from where I sat. The ambience was subdued with a warm glow about the place that diffused the chill outside.

It had been several weeks since we'd been able to meet, and I'd written up her tales and tantrums into new chapters. The book was beginning to take shape and I was quite pleased. It would, of course, need the requisite editing, as any book worth its salt does. That was a worry for another day.

As I twisted the stem of my glass, Marie's tale of being a dominatrix swirled again about my head. I'd wondered why she would attempt such a mad endeavour, but quickly followed that up with the question of why she gave up so easily! I decided that would be for the readers to work out, but the more I got to know her, the more I admired her persistence on achieving a life well lived.

I moved a stray strand of my hair behind my ear and looked up; Marie was walking towards me. As ever, she was self-possessed and looked full of confidence; looking better than anyone that close to fifty should do. Almost like an advert for hairspray, her long dark hair bounced around her slender neck, and a beige and red tartan pashmina was wrapped around her shoulders.

I stood as she approached the table, she unwrapped her pashmina, shook snowflakes from her hair and we exchanged a kiss on the cheeks.

"Well don't you look radiant," I offered.

"Oh, you think? I thought I'd spice it up and give my European manners some air!"

That explained the cheek kiss, I thought, having never exchanged something so French—or perhaps I should say Italian—with her before.

"Well, it's perfectly classy and suites you divinely," I said in a mock posh voice.

"You flatterer," Marie said with a wave of her hand, before repeating the same comment in Italian: "Mi lusingate!"

"And where is your dear husband this evening?" I enquired.

"Oh he 'ad a previous engagement with the telly and a certain football match," she replied, reverting to exaggerated Lancastrian.

I laughed as we both sat and I poured her a glass of Pinot Grigio.

"Cheers!" we both said and chinked glasses before she drank greedily.

"Bloody 'ell I needed that!"

"Do you fancy any food?"

"Oh I had a decent lunch thanks, I can't maintain my figure with food *and* drinks, so I'm settling for a bowl of grapes!"

I reached down and dug about a bit in my overly large and quite stuffed bag that lay on the floor next to me until I located the new recorder. I had finally upgraded to a digital and no longer required cassette tapes.

"We're getting closer and closer to the present I suppose, but knowing you I can imagine there's still more madness to come," I said as I fiddled with the new machine, looking for the record button.

"That's a fancy contraption you've got now!"

"I should have paid closer attention to the directions. Ah, here it is," I replied, but it was more of a quiet grumble to myself. Having succeeded in the task of hitting record, I placed the device in the middle of the small table.

"Ready to go?" I questioned, and she gave me an unusual look.

"I suppose I should be used to it now."

"You got a problem?"

"Oh don't worry and it's not that I haven't enjoyed our time together, me telling my story, the recorder quietly observing all your inquisitions, but I have to admit that sometimes I feel bit over exposed, a bit self-conscious about the whole thing."

"How do you mean?" I was a bit astonished. After her first reservations she'd been nothing but open.

"Oh it's not you so don't misunderstand me. Everyone thinks their life would make a good book, as have I, when considering all things that've happened, but I suppose I get the feeling of sharing too much at times."

I reached for the recorder, "Should I stop it?"

"Don't be silly, Tina. Keep recording, of course."

The recorder made a soft thump as I set it back down. My hand grabbed the stem of my glass and I brought the drink to my lips for a sip. As the wine gave me that brief buzz, I felt a tinge of guilt for any negative feelings Marie might be feeling. There was a gentle clank as I set the glass back on the wooden table.

"Now I'm feeling a bit...bad. That maybe I pushed you into..."

"No. No," Marie interrupted me. "I don't want you to take it personally. I came to each session knowing exactly what I wanted to say, ready to reveal, warts n'all! It's just that from time to time I wonder about it. Who will read the book? Will they judge me harshly? Will they relate to what I have to say? Will they...gasp...find me boring?"

"Hold it right there," I stopped her. "Let me allay your fears. No one will ever find you boring—don't consider that for a second—but I cannot promise they won't judge you harshly. If you get an audience wide enough to have harsh critics, I should consider that a good thing. There's nothing I can do about the feeling of exposure—and confessing to working in a dungeon would take some beating if you'll excuse the pun—but this book is... oh just 'right' to do."

"Yeah I guess," she said with a sheepish grin.

"Good! I want you to relax and know that when it's time to edit, you can see what it looks like spelled out and in print. You might want to add more details, but then you might want to delete a few things, but let's not put the cart before the horse eh?"

"You really think I'm not boring?" Her smile was entirely flirty. "You flatter me."

I couldn't help myself, I laughed.

"I suppose I'm just being silly," Marie said with a shake of her head.

"And I've been obtuse. Since we got going I've been so eager to hear the next chapter I didn't even consider your feelings about sharing it all anymore."

I glanced down at the recorder, red light aglow, and realized all of this was being recorded.

"What do you think if I added this conversation to the book?" I asked.

"What?" Marie said a bit loudly as shock played on her face.

"What do you think?" My voice was even and inquisitorial.

Marie looked down, a thoughtful expression on her face. She played with the condensation on her glass, considering my question.

"I think..." she said and paused. "That it is bloody brilliant."

"Good. All your tales are about you in the past, but I also want to share something of the woman today."

Our eyes met and hers flashed with a twinkle.

"I like that I can say I'm a bit nervous, but at the same time a bit proud. I like it."

"Great! Now...did you come prepared? What is it that happens next in the saga of Marie?"

Marie straightened her back, pushed her hair behind her shoulders and began.

"It's January 2006 and Grandma Alice was now in a nursing home in Rochdale. She was now in her 80's and had been living in a bungalow since Frank died some 15 or 16 years earlier. The doctor who insisted she was placed in a care home described her heart as a paper bag with no air in it and she just needed to be cared for in her last weeks. This time in my life was just heart breaking. I wanted so much just to ditch everything and rush down there but dad said it wasn't time yet so I waited." It was so obvious with Marie how much she adored her Grandma. She was remembering this like it was yesterday looking so sad.

"One night the house phone rang," she continued. "It was around 11pm and I shot out of bed waking John up fully expecting it to be dad to say Grandma had passed. I answered, out of breath from running down the stairs. It was the nursing home night staff! They said that Grandma was asking if she could speak to me urgently and was getting so upset. So they called me and put her on the phone. That call was absolutely heart rending Tina. She was begging me to take her to my house. She was crying and getting herself into a right state. I had to promise her I would pick her up the next day before she would go back to her room." At this point Marie burst into tears and left the room. I felt so sorry for her. Her Grandma was such a big part of her heart and that call must have been terrible for her being hundreds of miles away. "I managed to calm her down a bit and she gave the phone back to the night staff. I said for them to call me as soon as she was settled. They called me back 30 minutes later and said she was fine and asleep. Needless to say I couldn't sleep at all that night!"

"A few weeks later dad called to say I should come now. John didn't hesitate and told me to go straight away, that he would see to the kids. I packed a few bits and jumped into my car and started on the 3.5 hour journey to her. I've no idea where that time went. I was on auto pilot, just wanting to see her before she passed. When I arrived in the carpark it was dark. Mum and Dad were standing outside on the steps. They walked over to the car and I just knew........................I was too late. I threw the keys to my car away from me and sobbed. Dad grabbed me and pulled me out of the car and we 3 just hugged in that car park and cried for the woman who had meant so much."

"That must have been awful for you all Marie" I offered "Yes, it was just so sad. We went into the home and to her room. She looked so peaceful in her bed. She was a little cold but just looked asleep. My mum had put a blanket that I had made for her on top of her quilt which was a lovely thing to do. I still have that blanket. I also have her bible. It was given to me by Grandma herself and I have it locked away."

"How was your Dad? He was an only child wasn't he?" I asked.

"He was sad obviously, but he got on with funeral arrangements. My sister and I wrote a few words as a eulogy to read at the funeral and mum was busy arranging flowers etc. We actually went to see her in her casket. I'm so glad I did. Everyone let me go in on my own and I told her how much I loved her. She looked so beautiful in her favourite blue blouse, her slate grey hair combed back for her public appearance. Mum came in and kissed her forehead before putting a £20 note down by Grandmas hand. It was something she always did with us all. She would secretly put £20 in our hands when we visited so that Frank didn't see. It just carried on after he left us."

As Marie was telling me these memories her whole body language changed. It was so obvious she was grieving and still is for her Grandma.

"So the funeral day arrived," she sighed, "and we were to all meet at the funeral directors. A large crowd was there actually. All of our cousins and second cousins. Grandma's sister too, her brother had previously died. As we were asked to get in the family car I ended up sitting next to Dad and mum was in the row behind for some reason. When we set off behind Grandma at a snail's pace my dad got hold of my hand and squeezed it. It was so out of character for him that I looked at him a bit shocked. He was sobbing his heart out looking out of the window of the car. In that moment I had so much love for my Dad I could have burst. No words were needed, we just sobbed together for the duration of that long drive to Grandmas final resting place. She was to be buried with the man who whisked her away to Yorkshire and married her, Jim Turner. She once told me he was the only man she ever loved"

I stopped the recorder and held up my hand. I couldn't speak. Such was the heavy lump in my throat. I quietly left Marie alone for a few moments to compose myself.

"Ready to go on?" I asked when I entered the room again. "Yes, yes Tina. Sorry about that. I still get so upset remembering Dad in that car!" She said sadly. "Ok, so the Chapel where the service was held was packed. She was obviously very well liked in the community. My sister Helen and I were to read our Eulogy around half way through. We both got up, took our place behind the plinth and Helen started reading but she couldn't go through with it and sat down. I just fixed my eyes on my brother and read our words of respect to the end. Grandma was lowered into the freezing ground on top of Jim. We all sobbed then. It was over. Mum and Dad arranged for her name etc. to go on the grave stone and John and I make sure we visit the grave at least every 2 years. Some folk say it does nothing for them visiting a graveside but I find it therapeutic. I feel very close to Grandma when I go there."

Marie sniffed and wiped her eyes, taking a huge breath. "God I was dreading going through that bit," she laughed. "OK, let's get on with life after Grandma!"

The kids have got on a bit in age by now. I can hardly believe how time manages to give with one hand and steal with the other." She sighed and continued, "Our house was the same one in Dunfermline, cosy as it was. I did piercings from there and John was still a health and safety advisor. Louise, the dear child, was a nightmare... the Reactive Attachment Disorder. One minute you'd think she was a normal teenager doing normal things and then you'd discover everything she'd been saying is a lie. She'd lie about big things, sure, but a lot of it was insignificant. She'd say her favourite colour was blue when it was yellow, she'd say she loved a movie when she hated it, she'd say she was meeting friends when she was sitting alone reading. She was rather manipulative and sometimes argued over the smallest thing, mostly a lot of small stuff that took a lot of time to deal with. Millie got the short end of the stick when it came to my attention and when I could I'd send Louise to spend time with her dad. I still feel so bad and racked with guilt about Millie being side-lined all of the time"

"That's an interesting decision, sending Louise to Jacks."

"Yes, but there were the other children to think about; John's as well as Millie. She always came back sooner than she was supposed to though, Manchester not being the place for her despite her saying she was looking forward to it when she left. More lies. Jack had done some growing of his own and was much more of a responsible father, and Louise had chores to do. When she hadn't done things he caught her out with her lies and manipulations and strove to teach her lessons about them. Despite coming back too soon, I was pleased with the amount of maturing she did at Jack's sometimes."

"How old was she then?" I asked.

"Oh I guess about eighteen or nineteen. She was ready to play at being an adult and she got a job at a pet store. Then we started to look at flats for her."

"That's a lot of responsibility. She was ready for that?" I finished my drink and topped up our glasses.

"Quite honestly, it was sink or swim. Only one way to find out, right?"

"Push 'em out of the nest." I said.

"Something like that, but she really wanted it. And again I was thinking of the other children. Sure they were older and quite independent, but the amount of drama that girl caused... God it was a big relief to have her out of the house. But like I said, she'd matured, so really it was less of an issue.

"Anyway we managed to find a decent flat that was perfect for her. The others were either too horrible or out of her price range. Her new home was in an old Victorian house with huge windows that overlooked the countryside."

"That sounds lovely. Sounds like she really got lucky."

"Oh I agree. So, as Louise was getting all settled, I was talking to this friend called Dominic one day and he was telling me how stressed he was. He managed properties, but there were too many, over one hundred. I got it in my head that maybe he could hire me and I could help out. The piercing thing was coming to an end, there were new regulations about to take effect and they wouldn't allow me to work out of my home. I figured there wasn't anything to lose by jumping on this opportunity. I asked him if I could help him out.

"We had a bit of a discussion where he gave me a general idea of what the job would entail. I thought it sounded incredibly promising and I wanted to get my hands on it. It was two weeks before I heard from him, but actually it was Laura, his wife, that called me and we went from there. I started with their properties in Fife and received a percentage of the fees which came to a decent sum."

"What kind of work was it?" I asked.

"Nothing too intensive for the most part. It could get rather busy with the accumulation of small tasks. I showed prospective tenants the property and as my role grew there was banking, vetting, managing tenant issues, helping with housing benefits...boring bureaucratic stuff. But I was thrilled since there was a lot of opportunity for problem solving and I enjoyed that immensely.

"Dominic and Laura taught me a lot and they liked my work. We opened our own property management company and John even got in on it. They added ten properties to their portfolio and we managed them as well. It was rather thrilling to have such a successful endeavour and I enjoyed the money. Who wouldn't?"

She took a sip of her drink as I decided my self-control wasn't nearly as good as hers.

"I think I might get a plate of chips?" I said with a guilty grin and she laughed out loud.

"Chips? Oh Tina Piper! How do you manage your figure?"

"You must be joking?"

"Of course not! You're so slim and I could never get away with eating chips after carbs at lunch time."

I shrugged. I didn't think about my figure because there wasn't much of one to speak of. Though Marie was voluptuous and still embodied sex appeal, I suppose one sees oneself differently. I called a waitress over and put in my order and then we continued.

"In 2007 Louise got pregnant with her boyfriend Nick and gave birth to her son Peter later that year. The labour was hard; her temperature rose, the baby's heart rate fell, there was flurry of activity, doctors moving this way, nurses moving that way, and no one telling us a thing. Louise was put on drip for antibiotics and she was just out of her mind. For a bit we thought she was going to need an emergency caesarean but it didn't come to that. She began pushing though she was a bit on the delirious side. But Peter came out and he looked perfect. Nick was overcome with emotion and was proud to be a dad and I was thrilled to become a nana."

"The ultimate glamorous granny!" I suggested.

"As if! Anyway, Peter was placed on Louise's chest and as the cord was cut I was rather nervous that the RAD would make bonding hard as initially

Louise appeared to ignore the baby. But then it seemed to dawn on her that the baby was there and she started to give him tentative strokes on his head. God was I relieved!"

"Was Peter healthy?" I asked.

"Well he seemed the picture of a perfect healthy new-born, despite it transpiring that Louise had an infection. But everyone was pleased and Louise and the baby left the hospital the next morning. I took them home, but Nick was keen to show he was a proud dad and he took over care duties so that Louise could rest. After four days he returned to work so it was just me with Louise and Peter. The whole situation was just wonderful—my troubled daughter doing so well, my adorable grandson, and my property management business success."

"This is generally the part where the awful thing happens..." I ventured and Marie laughed.

"If I don't laugh, I'll positively break down in tears. Yeah you're right. Peter seemed to come down with a little cold, and it didn't seem like a big deal, but to be on the safe side we went to the doctor. The doctor diagnosed Peter with a cold and sent us on our way with a prescription for amoxicillin."

"That's odd," I said. "Antibiotics for a cold? I've never heard of that before."

The waitress brought my plate of chips and disappeared again before I could utter a thank you.

"Could I trouble you for one of those?" Marie asked with a lustful gaze.

"I'm more than happy to share the whole plate with you."

"Oh, cruel fates," she said as if doing Shakespeare and I cracked up as she added: "I will most likely have to take you up on your offer, you she-devil!"

We both ate for a moment before she nodded and wiped her fingers on a paper napkin.

"Where was I?" Marie said as she finished chewing. "Right, Peter's cold. Yes. Never have I heard of a five day old infant being given an antibiotic. Yet here we were. I was sceptical, but administered the first dose as prescribed and it seemed like it was working. He slept in his Moses basket and I took the opportunity to catch up on house work while Louise prepared his bottles.

"After a bit I checked on him and he just didn't look right. He was sweaty and rosy cheeked. When I picked him up he was like a rag doll and when I took his hat off I could see that his head had swollen."

"Oh bloody hell"

"Indeed. This was my grandson and if you ever have one you'll know what a scary feeling it is if they're seriously ill. We rushed him to A&E and he was admitted straight away into the children's ward. He was so tiny lying there and was so still and they weren't telling us anything.

"Eventually Nick showed up with his parents and John was there too and we all held vigil over little Peter. But so much time passed, and there just wasn't any news so everyone but me and Louise went home. She was encouraged to feed him, and she tried to coax him to take the bottle nipple but he just wouldn't suckle. They had to drip fluids into him with antibiotics and I thought it was so odd how he didn't even cry. There was not a peep from him and Louise could only cry and sleep and I was there with her for all of it. John was fantastic in a support role. My parents had moved to

Bulgaria of all places after the death of my beloved Grandma Alice so I just had to be strong for Louise.

"Day three came and the consultant was trailed by *seven* trainee doctors! He enquired as to how we could tell Peter was ill, and I explained everything that had happened, mentioning his swollen head. After thanking me he addressed his trainees by saying; "As with any meningitis infection................"

"What?" I couldn't help interrupting. "Is that really how you found out?"

"Exactly! So much for a caring doctor, the arrogant bastard. Louise and I exchanged stricken looks, and she ran out of the room crying as I stared at the doctor in disbelief. Peter had bacterial meningitis."

"God that's awful."

"I think then he realised they had handled the situation so poorly, and he tried to assure us they were doing everything they could. It was unknown how he got the infection, and the only thing they offered was that Louise's infection had probably 'not helped'. You think doctors are smart and know what they're doing. You wait. Get sick and see how much they don't know."

"I'll pass. Thanks."

"Smart lady. Anyway, I let the family know as difficult as it was, but Peter was the one suffering. He was isolated with IV drips and worst of all, lumbar punctures every two hours. Louise struggled to cope and she slept a lot after Nick took her home for a while, but John was my super hero as usual. He brought me some stuff so I could freshen up and then Nick's mum and I tag teamed and took turns staying with Peter."

"Was he improving?" I asked and she shook her head.

"He was having a bad reaction to the antibiotics, getting these nappy rashes with blisters. That poor tiny bum of his! We kept his nappy off for a bit and let his bum air out. Then, on top of everything, he was also diagnosed with E.coli. He was truly having a time of it and he was only 3 weeks old."

I just shook my head and a few tears trickled down her cheeks as she comforted herself with chips and wine. Eventually she swallowed deeply, wiped her face with the napkin and continued.

"Days wore on and we continued to take our turns being with Peter. Days turned to weeks and we started to see some progress. Feeding more, crying more, moving more, and I cried when he gripped my fingers while I fed him. It was this tiny thing that was so big. Then finally, the day came when he was discharged."

"That must have been such a relief." I offered.

"Well..."

"Oh no."

"Yes, well, nothing's ever easy is it?"

"I would say that none of that sounded easy." I said and she laughed wryly.

"I only offer stories that get more complicated, my dear. And this one? Why it's not any different. The same evening we were discharged he was re-admitted. This time? Viral meningitis. How did he get that you ask? No friggin clue. I told you. Get sick and find out how clueless our tireless army of doctors truly are. All of that education for "We don't know..."

"I just didn't know how we were going to get through another round of that. It was seclusion, IV drips and lumbar punctures over the course of several weeks again. It was tag teaming vigils, shock replaced by bouts of crying followed by sleeping. By the end of it all we were warned by the doctors of possible complications, and that Peter could experience behavioural problems, deafness, blindness, limb problems, and the list went on. But what did they know? Nothing that's what. Sure, these could crop up later, but we didn't care at that point. We were all ready to leave that wretched place and never turn back and finally, once more, we did. I was keen on having Peter and Louise at my house, but I had to let them go home and handle it on their own."

"I'm sure you were there to help."

"There's no denying that. I was there for the cuddles Louise could not give. I revelled in watching Peter meet his milestones, and each one was a victory: Hearing, sight, crawling, walking; he hit them all perfectly."

"Well that's encouraging."

"Oh I was so pleased, believe me. Then, when he was nine months, Nick and Louise split and she and the baby moved back home."

"Given all that had happened thus far, it hardly seems that tragic," I suggested and Marie gave a soft laugh.

"Anything was better than that damned hospital! However, Louise seemed even more detached and RAD was really rearing its ugly head. By this time she was living in another flat in a property I managed and that was good because I could visit."

"How was she getting on?"

"Badly. Her care for Peter was not all that it could be, nor her care for herself. I'd visit and she'd be comatose from drinking while Peter sat crying in his own filth. So dreadful. We were convinced that not only was she drinking but that she was on drugs as well. One night John decided that it would be better for Peter if we took him and when we got there we discovered Louise passed out in bed with a man. We told her that we weren't going to give him back."

"How did she react to that?"

"When she sobered up she called the police and we had to hand Peter over. Social services were bloody useless! We moved Louise closer to use so that we could keep watch over the situation. She was erratic, but we ensured Peter was well cared for so that made me happy.

"So life went on and then when Peter was around two and half years old Millie asked me to get something out of Louise's house. Millie had passed her exams and was off to University and I was immensely proud with equal measures of guilt. Louise stole all of my attention due to her demanding behaviour and independent Millie had just, well she had just got on with it!"

"So I was at Louise's house, but had Peter with me since I'd been babysitting him because Louise was out. As I was walking down the hall to find Millie's files Peter pointed at a missing bedroom door and said in his tiny little two year old voice, 'Penny hurt mummy.' I asked him what he meant, in the best way he could communicate he relayed that his mummy had a fight with her friend Penny, there were people drinking stuff, and there was loud music.

"Louise later revealed that she'd had a party and there were loads of teenagers including her friend Penny and her boyfriend. Penny got it into her head that Louise was trying to get with her boyfriend and chased her through the house. Louise locked herself in the room, but Penny broke the door down. She punched Louise over and over and wouldn't stop until a neighbour came over to pull the girl off Louise. He also said that Peter sat rocking himself in the corner and crying.

"I had seen the bruises on Louise's face, but she told me she fell down the stairs and I believed her. At this time Peter had been pooing in cupboards and we attributed this behaviour to his reaction to Louise's partying so we decided to take Peter away again."

"Did it work that time?"

"Not at all. Bloody useless social services again. We were told that as long as Peter was warm and fed there was nothing they could do. They had 'bigger' problems to deal with; whatever that meant. After what seemed like endless talking we convinced Louise to move in with us because we wanted to ensure that Peter was well cared for. Louise knew she was spiralling out of control and no one wanted to see that happen."

"Was Peter better then? Living in your house."

"In some ways yes, but then he started to display behaviours indicative of what's called a spectrum disorder—things like lining up his toy cars, not engaging in play, being withdrawn. But it was hard to give him all the time he needed because we were all still working, my Mum and Dad still in Bulgaria and my nephew was then diagnosed with life threatening aplastic anaemia."

"Good God!" I exclaimed.

At this point I noticed an increase in volume as the place was getting busier.

"We might consider going to a quieter place," I suggested. "At least for further recording."

"Well maybe, but I'm not leaving this table until that bottle is empty and these chips have disappeared."

"I agree," I said as I grabbed a chip.

EMAILS

Marie glanced at her reflection in the mirror by the front door, patting down some bits of fly-away hair and checked her lipstick.

"You look lovely," said John as he appeared in the living room doorway. He casually leaned on the frame with arms folded and appraised his wife.

Marie flashed him a weary smile.

"Don't be so nervous." John grasped her shoulders and gave her a kiss on my cheek. "Your client will be asleep anyway, so they won't know if you mess up!"

"Cheeky bugger!"

"Off you go then," John said as he went around her and pulled the front door open for her.

Marie put her bag on her shoulder and, with a wiggle of her shiny-nailed fingers, strutted out the front door and climbed into her car. As she fastened her seatbelt her phone dinged with a notification—a text from her nephew advising of a new job. She sent a quick congratulatory reply, and drove off with a small smile, remembering how he stuck through chemo. A memory of sitting by his bedside one dark night, surrounded by other family members, in a vigil for possibly his last moments of life, also came to mind. There was relief from all the family that he hadn't left them that night, and it continued as he grew stronger until the illness faded and he grew strong again.

Marie was heading towards her new rented office to hypnotize her first client. At a red light her phone dinged with again and she took a quick look—Louise had sent a picture of Peter sleeping in footie pyjamas and snuggling Louise's old blue teddy. The light turned green and Marie continued on her way with another smile. Peter's condition that suggested autism had turned out to be less severe than initially indicated and, with some help, he should grow to live mostly normal life. The family did seem more blessed these days and she hoped all would continue that way.

Car parked in her private place, she climbed the flight of stairs to her office. There was a plain reception area and no receptionist yet, but it was all hers. She went into her office and flicked the light switch, the dim glow revealing the second-hand sofa and a new chair from Ikea. It was still twenty minutes until her client was due, so she sat at her desk and pulled her laptop out of her bad. Time to check her emails

From: Ekrem22@gmail.com

Subject: Good luck.

Don't worry, dear. I know you are nervous but you are above all else talented. You will do well, beautiful lady.

Ekrem

Marie felt a warmth flood her chest. He'd remembered today was her first day. There was nothing else of interest, so she dived into Facebook and scrolled through the new posts. Louise's page was filled with Peter and photos of her teas and sweets and there were loads of likes and comments... nothing from Millie. She went directly to Millie's page and saw there was a bit of new information: In a relationship. Great! But it didn't say with who. Her timeline was devoid of any new posts in eighteen months... or perhaps Millie had blocked her from seeing them. At least she'd not been 'unfriended'.

There was a knock on the door and Marie went to her reception area where she greeted Mrs. "Call me Trudy" Turnbull; first hypnotherapy client.

Trudy was tall with long blonde hair straight out of a shampoo commercial. Her eyeliner was so sharp it could cut, and black eyelashes extended unnaturally long over chiselled cheek bones. Flowers blossomed with an explosion of garish colours all over a dress that accentuated her full figure with a cleavage you could stack a dinner plate in. She daintily grasped Marie's fingertips for a lady-like handshake that Marie felt was like greeting a lettuce leaf.

"I was rather pleased to find a hypnotherapist in my area. Thank god for Google," Trudy gushed as she walked into the reception area.

"Well I'm glad you did. Come this way," said Marie as she led her client to the private office.

"Have you just opened?" Trudy asked, in an affected a posh accent that reminded Marie of Hyacinth Bucket in *Keeping up Appearances*.

"I have and I'm just getting everything settled in. Shall we start?"

Trudy perched her ample rear on the edge of the sofa and Marie was glad she didn't disappear into it.

"Do I lie back?"

"In a moment, but first of all let's go over what you're specifically after and I'll explain how I'm going to help you accomplish that."

A little over an hour later Trudy dreamily exited her appointment with another one on the books.

Marie popped back on her computer and drafted an email to Ekrem.

It went really well! Thank you for your encouragement, this is exactly what I've needed. All that training to become a Hypnotherapist has paid off! The grind of the lettings management was just so...ugh. You know. Hugs and kisses, I'll talk to you later. Busy, busy, busy!

Grind. It was perhaps the right word, but sometimes it didn't say enough. She pulled out a stack of Easy Lettings paperwork. Her business partners had decided to part ways so it was just her and John. Was that becoming another grind? She was just getting started on the pile when her phone announced another text: John wondering how it went.

Marie: Good

John: Just good

Marie: More later. Dinner tonight?

John: Working late. You?

Marie: No. You'll eat out?

John: Probably

Marie sighed. Money was tight and John had to work late hours. Before she returned to the lettings paperwork she sent another email to Ekrem: Thinking about you.

After driving round and dealing with prospective and pain in the arse tenants for the rest of the day, when she walked in the door a little after six she was surprised by the smell of cooking.

"John?" she called as she put her stuff on the bottom of the stairs.

"Hi Mum!" Louise called from the kitchen.

"Hey you!"

Marie smiled as she walked into the kitchen and to see Louise helping Peter eat his chicken nuggets.

"What are you doing here?" Marie asked as she sat down. She made a point of not talking to Peter so she wouldn't distract him from eating.

"Can't a daughter pop in on her mum and make her dinner?"

"You've cooked? "I'm starving."

"Nothing special. Beef stew and tatties."

"Better than what I was gonna make. John's working."

Twenty minutes later, Marie had her own plate in front her, chatting to Louise while Peter played on the floor. She told Louise about her day and then they spoke about Louise's job at a branch of Frankie and Benny's. Louise was doing very well in front of house management.

"I'm right proud of you, you know that?"

"Thanks, mum," Louise said with a slightly embarrassed smile. They both knew what a shit she'd been in the past.

"Have you seen Millie's relationship status on Facebook?" Marie asked as she scraped the last of the stew onto her fork.

"Yeah. She's seeing some girl called Maisie."

"Hmm. Well. I haven't talked to her in a few weeks."

"She'll come around. She can't be mad at you forever."

Several hours later, John was still out and Marie headed to bed. She sat in bed with her laptop and was reading news articles when a new email popped up—Ekrem again. An hour passed of chatting and then Marie was getting too sleepy. She sent "hugs and kisses" and then slid into her covers and turned on a video on her laptop to fall asleep to. She supposed it was the one advantage to not having John in bed with her; she could use his space to set the laptop on.

The next morning she didn't need to rush out of bed for a hypnotherapy client, but she had plenty to work on for the Easy Lettings. John's side was empty and her laptop was also gone. Puzzled, she shuffled downstairs for morning tea and toast and found John sat at the table, laptop open.

"Did you come to bed last night?" Marie asked as she poured water in the kettle.

"I slept on the couch." John said. His voice distant.

"I would have moved over." Marie said. She grabbed a mug and her tea.

"I'm thinking you were wishing someone else was in bed with you."

"Huh?"

"Who's Ekrem?"

Marie's heart sank. Her chest burned and her stomach roiled. Suddenly she had no appetite for tea or toast.

"He's a mate online. We just chat..."

"Online mates don't end conversations with 'hugs and kisses'. I get one text about yesterday that says 'good' and he gets chapter and verse in a load of emails!"

Marie was silent. There was no retort she could think of.

"Have you done anything...in person?"

"No." Marie was quick to assure. "He's a Turkish guy, lives in Birmingham."

"Well...did you want to?"

"I'm...I...I don't think so. Maybe. I don't know."

John snapped the laptop lid shut.

"Sort it out, Marie."

Marie wanted to jump to her defence and question why he would take her laptop and snoop around in her private messages, but she realised it was a moot point. It was out there now.

"Well?" John asked.

"No. No."

"No what?"

"No I didn't want to do anything in person. It was just online chat. Nothing was meant by it."

John stared off in silence.

"What... what are you thinking, darling?"

"Don't. Don't you fucking dare. *He* called *you* 'darling'. You don't get to call me that."

With that John stood and walked out of the kitchen. She heard him having a shower and then the door slammed as he left for work. He didn't come back that night. The following day Marie had several hypnotherapy clients so was out of the house in her office. In between clients she checked her text messages.

John: I've grabbed some of my things. I won't be home for a few days. For the second time in her life she was experiencing raw heartbreak. What had she done?

Marie sent an email off to Ekrem letting him know that her husband had seen their messages and was very unhappy with the nature of their relationship. She told him she couldn't be in contact with him anymore. And in order to avoid any conversation with Ekrem, she blocked his email and his profile on Facebook.

Marie: Let's talk John. I've told him I won't talk to him anymore.

John didn't text back that day and after the last client she called his mobile. It went straight to voice mail. She didn't bother leaving a message.

The next week Marie struggled to maintain her work schedule not knowing what John was thinking. Her heart was mangled, thinking she'd destroyed her marriage. On Saturday afternoon, he came through the door when Marie was sitting on the sofa dealing with more paperwork.

She looked up at the sound of his entrance.

"Hey," she said and tried a smile. It wasn't returned as he sat in chair.

"You obviously don't want to be with me..."

"Shit John no! That's not it at all!"

"Really? And there's you merrily chattin' up some Turk!"

Marie slid the paperwork off her lap and scooted forward to kneel at his feet.

"We can work on our marriage," she tried, but John shook his head and broke eye contact.

"I've been thinking this week... the betrayal. It hurts too much. I'm going to petition for divorce."

"Hell John. No. We can fix this," she said, wondering whether she was going to throw up. John shook his head again.

"We've been through worse times. We've gotten through so much together."

Marie knew she was pleading and sounded pathetic, but it was all she could do.

"I' can't do it anymore," he said, easing past her to stand up. "I'll be back for my things." And he was gone.

Marie pulled back the curtain and watched him walk to his car and drive away. The sun was shining, but the pavement was wet from a recent rain. The trees had turned for autumn, but the leaves had yet to all fall. Paperwork suddenly seemed insignificant.

NEW BEGINNINGS

Marie walked out of one of the properties she managed and checked the time on her mobile—an hour before a therapy client. She hadn't heard from Millie in months and she sent her a text.

Marie: Hi

It wasn't much but she wanted Millie to know she was still around. She pocketed the mobile and headed to her office. At least all the effort of getting trained seemed to be paying off, but the family having that good luck she'd considered on her first day seemed to have otherwise fizzled out. At least Louise and Peter were happy.

As she sat at her laptop when her client had left, she relaxed for a while by reading through celebrity gossip in the Daily Mail. She had no urge to head back to her empty house. Louise popped up on Facebook Messenger.

Louise: John is on a dating site

Marie: How do you know?

Louise: uh...reasons. Here's the link

Marie pulled up John's profile and she was stunned. As in by a stun gun. Just absolutely gobsmacked. She couldn't even read anything at first. His image on a profile was all she could take in for nearly a minute, and then, as she read it, she began to break down and cry.

She eventually pulled herself together. Well sort of. She walked to the shop round the corner, she bought a bottle of coke and a Snickers and returned to the office. She got through one sip and one bite before she started crying again. What a stupid cow she'd been. She scrolled through more meaningless online crap to try to get her mind off John, and ended up falling asleep to a playlist of depressing music.

Easter was approaching and she sent Millie a card and an Easter basket filled with her favourite chocolates. Millie texted her back several times: 'Hi', 'I'm fine', 'Later'. That was it. Nothing about her life.

Marie walked in the front door, shopping bags in hand and the house reeked of silence as usual. She plopped the bags on the sofa and followed them. She hadn't been feeling right all day, her chest was tight and she was anxious. She had reasoned that it was the crowds at Tesco's shopping for the bank holiday weekend, putting her on edge with their aggressive attitudes, but now that she was home it felt worse. As well as her chest, her heartbeat was pounding, her hands shaking, and her head was light. As she leant her head back on the sofa, her vision was going dark around the edges and her breath increasing shallow. She fished around her stuff for her phone and managed to dial 999.

She woke up in a hospital bed hooked up to an IV drip and machines that beeped at even intervals. The curtain was pulled back and there stood John.

"Marie," he said, his voice tinged with panic.

She looked at his face as she tried to work out where she was and why. All she remembered clearly was the fat checkout girl at Tescos.

"John. What are you doing here?"

She tried to sit up, but got tangled in everything connected to her and her head swam a bit, but not as bad as before.

"Don't fuss," John admonished. "You're fine. The doctor said it was a panic attack and she said you'll be fine. The hospital. They called me."

John walked to Marie's bedside and gave her an awkward but relieved hug.

"You're squishing me," she said, her voice muffled through his shirt. God that felt good.

"Oh sorry." he said and pulled away. "Don't scare me like that again."

"I won't and..."

Her intended apology about everything was interrupted by the doctor, a tired looking woman in her mid-forties with deep forehead wrinkles. She flipped open Marie's chart and eyed it a second, before she asked how Marie was feeling. The answer was fine, just a bit tired. She was told she'd stay in for a night, but then she could go home. She'd be given a prescription for anti-anxiety medication.

"Is that what caused this? Anxiety?" John asked.

"Most likely. You'll want to follow up with your general doctor and see a psychiatrist."

"I'm loony. Is that it?" Marie questioned.

"It's normal these days to have panic attacks. There's not the stigma that used to be attached to mental issues."

"Did you hear that? You're mental." John teased.

"Well we already knew that. Didn't we?"

Two days later, Marie rounded the corner and stood in the doorway of the bathroom. John stood in front of the mirror with razor in hand and shaving cream smattered on his face.

"Did you take your medication?" John asked.

"Yeah."

"Are you sure?" John yelled.

"Yes. Don't worry. Have you got time for breakfast?

He nodded his head as he dragged the razor across his skin.

It was a trial—John moving back into the house. It was several days after the panic attack and Marie had paid a visit to a psychiatrist.

"You have some combined stressors; your marriage issues, your issues with Millie and you're working your butt off with those two jobs. It's bound to set anyone off." The psychiatrist had said.

Marie had pleaded with John that there was never anything between her and the Turk, and John agreed to give their marriage another chance while helping Marie. He took a bit of leave from work to manage the lettings and Marie cancelled the therapy clients in her books for the next two weeks. Were it not for John she'd have spent all day in bed. He pulled her out, tossed her in the shower, and forced her to do laundry, to cook meals for them, to watch TV at night. But she said she wasn't ready to leave the house.

Later that day it was a stormy summer afternoon, with lightning streaking across the black clouds. Marie had just finished a nap and rolled over in bed to the sight of John standing over her.

"Let's go to Tesco's," he insisted.

"But it's raining cats and bleedin' dogs out there!" She didn't say she hated the word 'Tescos' now.

She could hear the sheets of rain hitting her windows and the cracks of thunder.

"There are umbrellas and it's called a car. It's a wonderfully gloomy day to go to the store for some groceries."

"Huh," Marie protested, but sat up.

"Oh come on Marie. It's time and I'll be with you."

"Okay. But we're getting chocolate."

"Don't forget to get dressed."

"Lots of it."

"Seriously. Don't wear your pj's."

"Yeah Yeah."

John was sitting at the table in the kitchen when Marie walked in still wearing pj's.

"Well at least it got up,"

"Funny bugger," she replied, and then added more quietly, "Do I have to?"

"Yes and when's the last time you had a shower?"

"Do I smell that bad?" she asked and sniffed her arm pit.

"No but your hair looks greasy."

Marie fluffed her hair.

"Oh yeah. Probably three days."

"What? Up. Go."

John stood up and took her by the hand upstairs again.

"It's your fault, you're supposed to make me," Marie protested as John turned the water on and stripped her nightgown off.

He stood and watched the water fall down her back for a while and then she looked over her shoulder.

"Join me?" she asked, and her heart was fluttering. Please say yes.

He grinned and began to pull his t-shirt off.

It went on like this for another week, but each day Marie would feel a little better. John was there. He eventually had to go back to work and as she took over the Easy Lettings management again, maintained her meds, and started introducing therapy clients back into her work diet as she began to normalize.

The Ekrem incident didn't disappear, and John got to express his feelings of betrayal and Marie got to apologise. But John did accept that he'd been away with work too much and was inattentive to Marie. Marie thought maybe she was just trying to shake up her emotional life. There were never any plans to meet Ekrem.

After that their conversations veered towards what their future would look like together. Was it just going to be more of this for the rest of their lives? It was Louise who provided the key to change when she was offered a job at a flagship Frankie & Benny restaurant in London. She wanted to take it and was sure all would be OK—her employer was great about childcare support—but Marie was worried about Peter.

You smell good," he said as they lay in bed one night. She propped her leg on his as he played with her hair.

"I showered today."

"I know. I was there again."

Marie giggled and wiggled her fingers through his.

"I can't believe you'll be 55 next week!" Marie reminded him.

"I know, but I only look 35!

She laughed and hit him as she snuggled closer.

"Now there's an idea..." John muttered with a touch of revelation in his voice.

"What?" she asked, sitting up to face him.

"How about this?" he asked with a grin.

"What?"

"A solution to your worries about Peter."

It took 3 months to sort it all out, but by then John had cashed in the pension he could get his hands on at 55, and they'd sold the lettings business for a very good price. Their house had also been sold and they were on their way to London. The house they had there would be much smaller, but then they had a restaurant to buy as well.

EPILOGUE

FIVE YEARS LATER

The taxi pulled up to a closed gate. The taxi driver popped the boot and I moved around to the back of the car to retrieve my luggage.

"Well look what the cat dragged in!"

I turned around and there she was. I smiled at her and at the memory of her voice, one I not only listened to in hours of face-to-face conversations, but also hours of replaying the recordings, listening for nuances and hints of hidden emotions that I needed to draw out.

Marie greeted me with her arms wide open and we embraced for the first time in a year. She smelled like sunshine, vanilla, and a touch of sun cream. Her sunglasses were big, her blouse colourful, and her tanned feet bare beneath white linen trousers. I looked forward to getting into something cooler myself.

"It's been ages!" I said as we separated from our hug. "You positively glow."

"You are a delight to see," Marie said. "Let's get John to help with the luggage."

Before I could agree or refuse, she turned towards the villa and shouted, "John! Come and get Tina's luggage!"

"Yes m'lady!" came the reply from somewhere in the house.

Marie grinned and as she led me to the front door, I gazed up at the blue sky speckled with wispy clouds. I enjoyed the feeling of the warm air on my skin and followed her through the door and into a cool hallway.

"Down that way is the rooms," she said, pointing to her left, "the kitchen is straight ahead and here's the lounge."

She opened the door on her right into a sitting room. It was a simple space, with some sofas, a fireplace, and television. It was mostly painted white with some brighter-coloured artwork, but it had a very calm feeling about it, with the sea breezes coming in through the terrace doors. John appeared through the door behind us carrying my suitcase.

"Oh here's the bloody porter!" Marie said.

"Tina, so glad you could make it. What do you think?" John said as he too gave me a hug after leaving my suitcase by the door.

"Looks lovely! I'm very impressed. It's got a nice airy feeling."

"Better than smoggy London!" he replied.

Marie gave me a tour of her villa. Their newly-arrived current guests were out exploring for the afternoon so the house was quiet. I could smell the sea air all through the villa, along with the flowers from the garden. John was right about how different it was to London.

The floors were beige square tiles and my heels clicked on them as I trailed Marie while she proudly showcased her newest and most ambitious endeavour. I felt a bit of a thrill. It was like being inside my own book, the one that had been published some fourteen months previously. While I was with her when writing, the relationship had been different and she was on the inside and me on the out. Now she was being talked about in many magazines and that wasn't hurting my reputation. Her being on the TV had certainly helped.

She showed me a small room on the first floor I'd be staying in for my brief visit. Marie and John's room was down the hall from mine. My room had a view over the pool from the terrace and beyond that I could see the ocean. I sat on the bed and gave it a little bounce and we laughed.

"Don't you think you can bring any bloody Spanish waiters up here!" she said and I grinned.

After we finished the tour I went to my room to unpack and changed from jeans and London-cool sweater into a cotton dress, and padded barefooted out to the terrace on the ground floor at the rear of the villa. This overlooked the inviting kidney-shaped pool and we sat beneath an umbrella on wicker chairs with soft cushions

"John, be an angel and crack open a bottle will you?" she asked as John passed by the patio doors.

"Oh bloody waiter and porter is it?"

"Oh bugger off and I'll let you have a beer!"

John brought the drinks, a bottle of Pinot Grigio in an ice bucket for me and Marie and Estrella for himself. After the usual "cheers" we settled back to chat.

"So, miss London do you?" I asked.

"Here she goes with her bloody questions as usual!" she replied, her eyes twinkling over the top of her wine glass.

"It's the only chance I get to talk and shut you up for a minute!"

"Ha bloody ha!"

"Well do you?

Marie dropped her grin as she lowered her glass to the table.

"Well we miss Louise and Peter, and Millie and Maisie of course" she replied, "but we're glad to have got out of the restaurant business. Five years was enough."

"Aye and the climate's a damn site better!" added John.

The book had taken a year in the end and they had been four years into the venture when I met Marie in Bali. Towards the end of the time when I was gathering all the background for the book, they were both making noises about something new. We'd discussed putting their move to London and settling down there into the story, but had decided to leave it where they were leaving Scotland. As I was finishing everything off, they decided to move to Spain to rent a villa that they would live in, but also offer holiday accommodation. They were doing very well.

As we chatted more around their decision to leave and the sale of the restaurant, it felt strange being with Marie, but not interrogating her with my little tape machine. So many days and well into the night I spent with the recordings, at first transcribing them before building the narrative that is her life into cohesive chapters.

Once the book was published, the reviews were slow to come in at first, but when they did they were glowing. There was your usual 'it sucked', 'don't read', and 'not worth the money' reviews from incoherent trolls of course, but there's not much one can do to avoid that. Mostly it was good and then the women's magazines started taking more interest in us both.

My previous writing had been strictly fiction, but with Marie I had to be true to her essence and her experiences. I couldn't add in an explosion on a yacht or a love scene on the beach, although she had suggested we could. I'd resisted and I was now pleased I had. Losing her virginity with her arse to the stars was all the sex the book needed. There wasn't even any when she was in the dungeon.

"The pool looks so inviting." I said eventually.

"Do you fancy a swim later?" Marie asked. "It's nicer when the sun's warmed the water, but it's not so hot out of it."

John downed the last of his beer and stood up.

"I have some things to sort out. I'll catch up with you two later," John said and kissed the top of Marie's head before he disappeared back into the house.

"There's always something to do," Marie said.

"I would imagine, being your home and your business. Always must be tidy!"

"Oh God! The guests do get bloody messy at times! Yeah, there is lots to do, but it's a bit lonely sometimes if I'm being honest."

"Really?" She'd surprised me with how she'd just dropped it out, and then I guessed that she'd planned to. Something she wanted to talk about.

"Tell me more... "I added, with my own grin hidden behind my glass.

"Oh piss off! God, that brings back so many memories," Marie laughed. "Sitting across from you, telling you my life, like you're my bloody therapist."

"I don't have a degree in psychology, but I feel like I have a degree in Marie-ology," I said and Marie laughed again.

"I bet!" she replied as I pushed away my glass. Too early for too much.

"So, lonely. Is that you wishing for home then?" I asked.

Marie gave a thoughtful expression before answering.

"John's more settled, but I do miss the UK. I Skype Louise and Peter often – Millie will do more than text a few words sometimes - but it's not like actually having them around. I'm missing his growing years."

"Yeah I bet that's tough."

"It's also just so damned quiet. I miss meeting up with my friends and there's no kids! After years of mine, John's and Peter, the house is devoid of the clatter of kids all chirping for attention."

"So... plans on heading back?"

"Plans? No. Wishes. Maybe."

"You do seem so happy here."

"Oh I'm alright mostly and it's been a spectacular adventure. I'll happily admit to that. So you did watch us on TV didn't you?"

For three months as they settled in, John and Marie were stars of a TV show about people getting a new life in the sun. The book had attracted the producers since that pushed their ratings up, and me and Marie were dead happy because that certainly boosted sales.

"I did of course. It was fun to watch, but I just wish it could have been a chapter or two in the book. It amused me no end."

Marie grinned as she took a sip from her glass.

"We've expanded you know. We have some other places - called fincas here - that we let to holiday makers. They're adorable and cosy."

"You seem to be doing so well, but I do sense your apprehension still."

"Oh we are and it's not apprehension really. As well as family, I just miss being social as much as I was back home. The guests help sometimes, but you know they're different every week. I miss going out with me mates. All I get to do here is go to a bar and they're often full of old men. Not even much eye candy!"

"Right," was all I offered.

I wasn't trying to get her to tell me more like before. I could see she was pensive and I left her to it. She held her glass with a manicured hand on her knee, and she fidgeted with her foot. When she spoke again, she'd brightened.

"But we have had some laughs, like when we first arrived in Spain. The bloody sat nav sent us down the wrong way into a tiny alley way and we burned the clutch up in our new Insignia while the villagers were enjoying the spectacle."

"I enjoyed the spectacle as well," I said with a grin.

"The film crew caught it all. I was so embarrassed. And all my friends could see just how much we were succeeding in Spain," Marie laughed.

"It made for good TV," I grinned.

"Yeah if you're not in it! We managed to get it out and after a while the clutch seemed OK and we at last found the apartment that was to be our home for the next seven weeks. We dumped everything, filmed for a bit then found the nearest bar! During that time we made it our business to recce the area, get our Spanish residencies sorted out, filming, getting the villa holiday business online and started taking bookings. All was going great and at last we got the keys for the villa on the 1st. We hit the ground running because our first guests arrived on the 3rd!

"Baptism of fire."

"Yeah but they were lovely people, came from Wigan so had a lot in common to talk about. Although we were busy and making money from the off - which was good- I wasn't (and I am still not) 'feeling it'. Never happy.com!"

"You know, it seems like you put so much effort into your endeavours; the research, learning new skills, setting up the operation, and then once you've created something successful you're ready to move onto the next thing."

"You might be onto something there," Marie said with a laugh in her voice, "but at least we managed to stick with the restaurant for five years. It's like the thrill of the chase and I do get a bit of a kick out learning new things." She smiled before lifting her glass to her lips.

"Well I couldn't be more pleased to be here," I said.

"Of course! I'm delightful to be around!"

"Of course you are," I agreed with a smirk.

"No, don't *you* forget it," she said and we both laughed.

"I won't," I assured her.

"So, it has been a good move overall?"

"Yeah it has. When we found this place we knew we had to have it. We had to go through selling the restaurant and we've rented the house out in London, but I was just itching to get my hands on this place. As I said, we were getting bookings almost instantly. Then we added the other places and we're just booked through the season in all of those as well. Have you read our reviews online? Everyone has such lovely things to say about staying here. And now we're starting to see the same guests come back. I'll admit that pleases me."

"You know what this sounds like?" I asked.

"What?"

"Sounds like you may have another book in you. I'm thinking sequel. Marie: part two. London, Spain and maybe Paris next!"

Marie laughed, "Ha, I don't think so and that's to the book and Paris. I'm done putting my life on public display for the time being, and I'm not a fan of frogs!"

"Well you know where to find me if you change your mind. And it could be Italy instead."

She looked up, startled at first and then there was that sparkle in her eyes again.

"Now there's an idea..."

From the bottom of my heart I thank you for reading my story. I am sure that some of you readers will see similarities in our lives! My journey on this roller coaster of a life on Earth continues and the second book is being written now, watch this space, my family is going through something massive as we speak! Live is never quiet for us □

You can find me on Facebook: Donna Riseborough (Moss Black) in Dunfermline or Tina M Piper Author. You can also find me on Twitter at @donz1966 and Instagram donnam66.

I would love to hear from you.

Until next time...

30493727R00162

Printed in Great Britain
by Amazon